HAVE WE MISSED THE SECOND COMING?

A Critique of the Hyper-preterist Error

HAVE WE MISSED THE SECOND COMING?

A Critique of the Hyper-preterist Error

Kenneth L. Gentry, Jr., Th.D.

Fountain Inn, South Carolina 29644

"Proclaiming the kingdom of God and teaching those things which concern the Lord Jesus Christ, with all confidence."
(Acts 28:31)

Have We Missed the Second Coming?
A Critique of the Hyper-preterist Error

Material used in chapter 6 is used by permission. It was originally published in Keith L. Mathison, ed., *When Shall These Things Be?* as Chapter 1: "The Historical Problem of Hyper-Preterism" by Kenneth L Gentry Jr. (ISBN 978-0-87552-552-5). This book was published by P&R Publishing Co., P.O. Box 817, Phillipsburg, N.J. 08865 copyright 2004.

Published by Victorious Hope Publishing
P.O. Box 1874
Fountain Inn, South Carolina 29644

Website: www.VictoriousHope.com

Printed in the United States of America

ISBN 978-0-9826206-8-7

Victorious Hope Publishing is committed to producing Christian educational materials for promoting the whole Bible for the whole of life. We are conservative, evangelical, and Reformed and are committed to the doctrinal formulation found in the Westminster Standards.

Dedicated to

R. C. Sproul

in appreciation for his work in
orthodox preterism

LIST OF ABBREVIATIONS

BAGD	Bauer, Walter, William F. Arndt, F. Wilbur Gingrich, and Frederick W. Danker, *A Greek-English Lexicon of the New Testament and Other Early Christian Literature.* 3d. Ed.: Chicago: University of Chicago Press, 1979.
BDT	Taylor, Richard S., ed. *Beacon Dictionary of Theology*. Kansas City: Beacon Hill, 1983.
BKC	Walvoord, John F. and Roy B. Zuck, eds. *The Bible Knowledge Commentary: Old Testament* and *New Testament*. 2 vols. Wheaton: Victor, 1983, 1985.
CBTEL	McClintock, John and James Strong, *Cyclopedia of Biblical, Theological, and Ecclesiastical Literature.* 12 vols. New York: Harper and Bros, 1867-87; rep. Grand Rapids: Baker, 1981.
CEOED	Coleridge, Herbert, Frederick James Furnivall, James Murray, and Charles Talbut Onions, eds. *The Compact Edition of the Oxford English Dictionary*. 2 vols. Oxford: Oxford University Press, 1971.
DBI	Coggins, R. J. and J. L. Houlden, eds. *Dictionary of Biblical Interpretation*. London: SCM, 1990.
DHT	Hart, Trevor A. ed., *Dictionary of Historical Theology*. Grand Rapids: Eerdmans, 2000.
DJBP	Neusner, Jacob, ed. *Dictionary of Judaism in the Biblical Period.* Peabody, Mass.: Hendrickson, 1996.
DPT	Couch, Mal, ed. *Dictionary of Premillennial Theology.* Grand Rapids: Kregel, 1996.

EBC	Guthrie, Donald and J. A. Motyer, eds. *The Eerdmans Bible Commentary*. 3d. ed.: Grand Rapids: Eerdmans, 1970.
EDNT	Balz, Horst Balz and Gerhard M. Schneider, eds. *Exegetical Dictionary of the New Testament*. Grand Rapids: Eerdmans, 2004.
EDT	Elwell, Walter A. ed. *Evangelical Dictionary of Theology*. Grand Rapids: Baker, 1984.
ERF	McKim, Donald K. ed. *Encyclopedia of the Reformed Faith*. Louisville: Westminster, 1997.
HCC	Schaff, Philip. *History of the Christian Church*. Grand Rapids: Eerdmans, rep. n.d. (1910).
ISBE (1982)	Bromiley, Geoffrey W., ed. *The International Standard Bible Encyclopedia*. 4 vols. 2d ed. Grand Rapids: Eerdmans, 1982.
ISBE (1929)	Orr, James. "Apostles' Creed" in James Orr and John Nuelson, eds., *International Standard Bible Encyclopedia* Grand Rapids: Eerdmans, 1929.
MHT	Enns, Paul, ed. *Moody Handbook of Theology*. Chicago: Moody Press, 1989.
NDT	Ferguson, Sinclair B., David F. Wright, and J. I. Packer, eds. *New Dictionary of Theology*. Downers Grove, Ill: Inter-Varsity, 1988.
NIBD	Lockyer, Sr., Herbert, ed. *Nelson's Illustrated Bible Dictionary*. Nashville, Tenn.: Thomas Nelson, 1986.
NNCD	Kurian, George Thomas, ed. *Nelson's New Christian Dictionary*. Nashville: Nelson, 2001.
PEBP	LaHaye, Tim and Ed Hindson, ed. *The Popular Encyclopedia of Bible Prophecy*. Eugene, Ore.: Harvest House, 2004.

PKH	Walvoord, John F. *Prophecy Knowledge Handbook*. Wheaton, Ill.: Victor, 1990.
PSB	LaHaye, Tim. *Prophecy Study Bible*. Chattanooga: AMG, 2001.
RelEnc	Schaff, Philip, ed., *A Religious Encyclopedia or Dictionary of Biblical, Historical, Doctrinal, and Practical Theology*. 3 vols. Chicago: Funk & Wagnalls, 1887.
WDCT	Richardson, Alan and Alan Bowden, eds. *The Westminster Dictionary of Christian Theology*. Philadelphia: Westminster, 1983.
WDT	Harrison, Everett F., Geoffrey W. Bromiley, and Carl F. H. Henry, eds. *Wycliffe Dictionary of Theology*. Peabody, Mass.: Hendrikson, 1960.
ZPEB	Tenney, Merrill C. and Steven Barabas eds. *The Zondervan Pictorial Encyclopedia of the Bible*. Grand Rapids: Zondervan, 1976.

PREFACE

You may not have heard of the Hyper-preterist movement. Perhaps the main title of this book intrigued you: *Have We Missed the Second Coming?* Sounds absurd! Then you began to wonder about its subtitle: *A Critique of the Hyper-preterist Error.* What in the world is "Hyper-preterism"? It obviously is somehow related to "preterism." But now you must ask: What is "preterism"?

Though you may not be aware of Hyper-preterism, you could soon become rudely introduced to it. If you are in an evangelical church, you could soon experience the doctrine invading your church, disorienting its members, and disrupting its peace. Ignorance is *not* bliss. When you are blind-sided, what you don't know, *can* hurt you.

In the last thirty years the Hyper-preterist movement has made its presence felt in a number of evangelical churches. But it has an especially strong Internet presence that is able to attract theological enthusiasts. In fact, it is largely through its Internet presence that it has been able to grow in numbers, spread in geography, and infiltrate in churches.

I am an evangelical Christian pastor as well as an author. I have pastored for almost four decades and have written many articles and books in the field of biblical prophecy. Because of these forms of ministry, I receive a fairly regular flow of correspondence asking for my thoughts on Hyper-preterism and seeking my counsel for handling the problem in churches. When I pastored in California I even had one Christian bookstore owner ask me how to get a particular Hyper-preterist to quit loitering in his bookstore each day where he would corner and challenge people on this matter.

Because of these frequent questions, I have decided to publish this book as a brief summary and critique of the Hyper-preterist system. I will not engage the full system in all of its many variations and intricate subtleties. There are too many variations and too much infighting in the movement to provide a full critique in a book this size. Wherever you have five Hyper-preterists, you may have seven or eight different views, for occasionally a Hyper-preterist will not even agree with himself.

The material within is of a basic and introductory nature. It is for those who are either altogether unaware of the Hyper-preterist movement and its dangers, or who have only recently been alerted to its existence and are wondering what it is all about. I hope that despite its brevity this work will at least awaken Christians to a few of the theological and exegetical errors within this novel re-interpretation of Christianity.

This book is basically a collection of materials on the subject that I have published in other contexts — though with some tweaking. Because of the collected nature of this work, you will note some repetition in certain places. Yet since repetition is an important tool of learning, this should be helpful rather than distracting.

Though Hyper-preterism is a new theological construct in evangelical circles, it has developed a rather enthusiastic and often combative body of followers. What they lack in numbers, they more than make up for in noise. Though this movement is known by its critics as "Hyper-preterism," its advocates generally prefer to call their theology "full preterism," "consistent preterism," or even simply "preterism." (The last tendency hijacks an historically accepted term, fills it with new content, and employs it for a new purpose.)

I would like to thank Mischelle Sandowich for her proof-reading the manuscript. She has a keen eye. I hope my eye is as keen in catching all of her many notes and recommendations!

So once again, you are probably asking: What *is* preterism? In chapter 1 I will provide a brief introduction to the system and remind Christians of the significance of the basic doctrines that it undermines. But now, let us get started!

Chapter 1
THE PRETERIST SYSTEM INTRODUCED

Christians rightly understand that prophecy is an important issue in Scripture. But they generally do not realize that it is also a deep and complicated one. Too many evangelical Christians today approach prophecy naively, looking at the Bible as if it were a jig-saw puzzle to play with. Sadly an enormous market exists for those who engage biblical prophecy in this manner.

One deficiency latent in such Christian naivete is the tendency not to recognize that several types of prophetic discourse exist in Scripture. Biblical eschatology is not "cut and dried." The particular approach which interests us in the current inquiry regards: *preterism*. If you do not know what preterism is, you certainly will not know what *Hyper*-preterism is.

So then: what *is* preterism? One of the most basic methods for detecting counterfeit money, is to be fully familiar with the look and feel of legal money. Similarly to be able to recognize *Hyper*-preterism, you must first understand what *orthodox* "preterism" is. Only then will you be in a position to see how Hyper-preterism makes its mis-steps.

So now: what is orthodox "preterism"?

Preterism

The term "preterism" derives from the Latin *preteritus*, which means "gone by, past."[1] The orthodox preterist sees certain prophetic passages that many believe apply to our approaching future as having *already* been fulfilled in our distant past. Hence, those particular prophecies are *preteristically* understood: their time in history is "gone by, past."

All Christians are ultimately preterists

Here I would note that *all* evangelicals are preteristic to *some* degree. After all, *some* New Testament prophecies clearly have been fulfilled. For instance, Jesus cites Old Testament prophecy and then uses it to make his own prophecy about his approaching death: "The Son of Man is to go, *just*

---

[1] CEOED 2:1330.

as it is written of Him; but woe to that man by whom the Son of Man is betrayed!" (Matt 26:24; cp., Matt 17:12; 20:18; 26:2).

Clearly Jesus' statement in Matthew 26:24 is a *prophetic* pronouncement: it presents a future event that is to transpire in history. And therefore, just as clearly, we today must recognize it as a *preteristic* prophecy. This is because we all understand that it has been fulfilled — in Passion Week in the first century almost 2000 years ago. Thus, this prophecy must be understood *preteristically*, as "gone by, past."

Other passages, though, cause confusion and debate among Christians. Orthodox preterists recognize important near-term indicators in several New Testament prophecies, which move them to declare these as examples of preterism. Let me illustrate this from a highly-debated sample. Though this prophetic sample is much debated, either view of it falls within historic, Christian orthodoxy.

In Matthew 24 we find the Lord's Olivet Discourse, which warns of "wars and rumors of wars" (Matt 24:6), "famines and earthquakes" (Matt 24:7), "false prophets" who "will mislead many" (Matt 24:11), the "abomination of desolation" (Matt 24:15), "the great tribulation" (Matt 24:21), "false Christs" (Matt 24:24), and more.

When does Jesus teach that these things will occur? Is he prophesying *our* future today, hundreds of years after his original prophecy? Or is he warning of events to occur in the near-term future of his own day, in the time of his original hearers? The two most basic answers given by evangelicals are rooted in either futurism (i.e., it will happen in our *future*) or preterism (i.e., it happened in our *past*). The futurist interpretation is well-known, being the position of many best-selling Christian books, such as *The Late Great Planet Earth* and the *Left Behind* series. But what about the preterist approach?

The preterist points out that in the very context where Jesus utters these warnings, he concludes: "Truly I say to you, this generation will not pass away until all these things take place" (Matt 24:34). He dogmatically declares ("truly") that this prophecy is to transpire in "this generation" — his generation, the one that he is addressing (Matt 23:37–38), the one that includes those who asked the question that sparked the Discourse (Matt 24:1–3). How could his original hearers understand anything else?

A number of such near-term passages are scattered throughout the New Testament. Before I expand on a few of these, however, I will highlight some of the dangers of hyperpreterism.

All Hyper-preterists are theologically dangerous

In the case of Hyper-preterism, however, its advocates see *all* prophecy as having been fulfilled before the end of the first century. These prophecies come to pass by AD 70, the year in which the Jewish temple was destroyed. Hence, their system is *Hyper*-preterism.

The adjective "hyper" speaks of excess, exaggeration. We see this meaning in the word "hyperbole" (which literally means "to throw back in an exaggerated way: *bole* is the Greek word for "throw"). Their preferred labels, though, include "full preterism" or "consistent preterism." But as an orthodox preterist, I prefer to label their recent innovative theology "Hyper-preterism." I believe that they have taken a true principle of Scripture (preterism) and pushed it beyond its biblical limits; hence, it becomes *Hyper*-preterism. This, of course, leads them to reject the orthodox view as "inconsistent preterism" or "partial preterism."

Be careful, though, that you not write-off the Hyper-preterist view too quickly as absurd and unwarranted — and therefore not necessary to understand. You must realize that they do have texts from which they attempt to derive their systems. In this regard they are similar to Jehovah's Witnesses and Mormons: they can point to biblical texts that *seem* to affirm their position. And if you are not alert to these, you may become confused when you try to rebut them.

One key text Hyper-preterists see as foundational to their system is Jesus' prophecy regarding the coming destruction of Jerusalem. In Luke 21:20–24 the Lord declares that Jerusalem will be surrounded and desolated. And in this important passage we find him also asserting in v. 22 that: "these are days of vengeance, so that *all things which are written* will be fulfilled." Note well: Jesus states that "all things" which are written are to be fulfilled when Jerusalem is surrounded and destroyed. How would you answer the Hyper-preterist on this point?

I will focus on Luke 21:22 later in the book (chapter 3). But for now, I am simply noting that this passage is a key element for the Hyper-preterist perspective on prophetic fulfillment. And I hope to alert you to the fact that they have several points-of-departure in the New Testament that you must recognize and understand. To be forewarned is to be forearmed.[2] If you are not ready for such Scriptures, you may be over

---

[2] The Sixteenth Century Latin phrase loosely translated thus was: *praemonitus, praemunitus*. The 1592 work by Robert Greene's *A Notable Discovery of Coosnage* put the matter poetically and effectively: "forewarned, forearmed:

whelmed by the apparent flood of arguments they present. You will be like those in the days of Noah: "they did not understand until the flood came and took them all away" (Matt 24:39).

Some of the prophecies which Hyper-preterists deem already fulfilled radically impact several important doctrines of the church. They believe, for instance, that the second advent of Christ and the resurrection of the dead were fulfilled in the first-century.

In fact, because they see *all* prophecy as having been fulfilled in the events leading up to and surrounding the AD 70 destruction of the temple, Hyper-preterists also argue that history will *never* end, that the world in which we live will exist forever and ever. They argue this by programmatic and logical necessity: if Scripture teaches that history will end, then at least this one prophecy would remain unfulfilled. As a result of such a commitment, they are in significant conflict with the whole of historic, orthodox, evangelical eschatology, as well as with many areas of its broader theology.

As already indicated, I myself am a preterist — but I am a preterist in the traditional sense of the term. My preterism is fully orthodox in all of its theological commitments and implications. I find many of the positions of Hyper-preterism to be heretical in denying several of the basic doctrines of historic orthodoxy.

I generally deem my preterism to be *exegetical* preterism. This is because I am led to a preterist analysis due to specific, clear statements in the text of the New Testament. Thus, exegesis leads me to preterism. But I see Hyper-preterism as *theological* preterism. Hyper-preterists have developed a whole new, alien system of theology by forcing preterism onto texts where it is not required. Consequently, my preterism is a *hermeneutic tool* for understanding many passages of Scripture, whereas Hyper-preterism is a whole *theological system* controlling all passages of Scripture.

But *why* is the matter so important? We recognize differences and accept debates between dispensationalists, premillennialists, amillennialists, and postmillennialists without charges of heresy. And some of these differences are quite large: will Christ return before the millennium or after it? Will evil increase toward the end or righteousness? Is Christ's

burnt children dread the fire."

reign to be physically conducted from Jerusalem or spiritually from the Jerusalem above?

The differences we have with Hyper-preterists, however, are much larger. And they are of a different order altogether. So here I will indicate why I believe the matter is so significant. I will briefly focus on the second advent as a cornerstone of evangelical theology. I do this for two reasons: (1) To encourage Christians to recognize the importance of the Lord's second coming (it is a non-negotiable doctrine), and (2) to demonstrate that orthodox preterism itself is an acceptable evangelical option.

Sadly, many who oppose preterism fail to distinguish between its use and its abuse, between the orthodox system and its heterodox perversion, between orthodox preterism and Hyper-preterism. In fact, they often criticize me, thinking that my preterism is simply another form of Hyper-preterism. So as an orthodox preterist I want to briefly consider the significance of:

The Second Coming

I believe Christ is coming again in the future — visibly and bodily, in great glory and power. Unfortunately though, too many Bible students overlook the different *ways* in which the Bible can speak of Christ as coming. This oversight can cause confusion in trying to interpret the New Testament — because one of these comings is actually a metaphor for the divine judgment befalling Israel in AD 70. Yet Hyper-preterists elevate this imagery as the second coming, thereby supplanting historic orthodoxy in this regard.

The misunderstanding regarding the various ways in which Christ "comes" is especially rampant among prophetic populists. But we must understand that not all biblical references to the Lord's "coming" refer to the second advent in the future. This is an important qualification that I must note before I highlight the second advent itself.

The various comings of Christ

Among the various ways in which Scripture speaks of Christ's coming, we may briefly list the following.

His spiritual coming. Christ comes spiritually to each individual believer *in the Holy Spirit's ministry*. He expressly teaches this when he says: "I will pray the Father, and He will give you another Helper, that He may abide with you forever; that is the Spirit of truth.... I will not leave you orphans; I will *come* to you" (John 14:16, 18, cf. vv. 23, 28). Since he is with his disciples in this context, it speaks of the Spirit's indwelling of the born-again believer which will begin at Pentecost (Acts 1:5; 2:16).

After the initial outpouring of the Holy Spirit upon the church, though, this coming of Christ by his Spirit occurs at the moment of salvation of each individual — for no Christian is without the Holy Spirit (Rom 8:9; 1 Pet 1:11). For instance, Paul writes: "He saved us, not on the basis of deeds which we have done in righteousness, but according to His mercy, by the washing of regeneration and renewing by the Holy Spirit, whom He poured out upon us richly through Jesus Christ our Savior" (Tit 3:5–6). Elsewhere he states regarding the new believer that he is "strengthened with power through His Spirit in the inner man, so that Christ may dwell in your hearts through faith" (Eph 3:16–17).

We must understand that those *not* saved by God's grace are by definition "without Christ" (Eph 2:12; cp. Rom 8:9).[3] Thus, Christ is not *with* them; he has not *come* to them. Therefore, salvation involves a spiritual "coming" of Christ into a person's life to save him from his sins.

His fellowship coming. Christ also "comes" spiritually to believers *in fellowship* as they worship and serve him. As he tells the sinful church at Laodicea: "Behold, I stand at the door and knock. If anyone hears My voice and opens the door, I will *come* in to him and dine with him, and he with Me" (Rev 3:20). Dining is a particular means of and therefore a potent symbol of fellowship (Gen 43:16; Matt 8:11; 9:10; 1 Cor 5:11; Gal 2:12). The members of the Laodicean church "are neither cold nor hot" (Rev 3:15). But Christ desires their fellowship and a warm relationship with them. Therefore he seeks to *come* in among them to dine.

His worship coming. Jesus "comes" among his people spiritually *as they worship together before Him*. "For where two or three are gathered together in My name, I am there in the midst of them" (Matt 18:20).[4] Though the word "come" does not appear in this reference, it is necessarily implied. For wherever two or three are *not* gathered together in his name, he is *not* present in this sense.

---

[3] See also: Mark 4:11; 1 Cor 5:12–13; Col 4:5; 1 Thess 4:12; 1 Tim 3:7; cf. John 15:1–7.

[4] Though this passage is specifically speaking of Christ's presence in church discipline, it is the church gathered in worship that disciplines. Consequently, it teaches that Christ is among the church gathered. In fact, he is simply applying a general principle to a specific church issue.

Christ, therefore, "comes" among his worshiping people in a special, holy, corporate sense that differs from his coming in regenerative salvation and individual fellowship. When fully understood this heightens the spirituality and seriousness of worship. But for our present purpose it demonstrates another way in which Christ comes.

His coming at death. Jesus comes spiritually to *believers at death*. "If I go and prepare a place for you, I will *come* again and receive you to Myself; that where I am, there you may be also" (John 14:3). We know that the disciples (and other believers since then) enter into heaven to be with the Lord at their deaths (Phil 1:21–23; 2 Cor 5:6–9). Hence, this statement must mean he comes to them *at their deaths* — otherwise, where have the disciples been for 2000 years?

Though Stephen's death is unique in Scripture, it indicates something of the personal involvement of Christ in the decease of all his saints. The Lord appears to Stephen as he dies in order to "receive" him (Acts 7:55–56, 59). Christians are not left to find their way to heaven when they die. Christ spiritually *comes* to receive us into the presence of the Father.

His exaltation coming. Christ *comes* into the presence of the Father *at his ascension*, in order to receive his mediatorial kingdom. "I was watching in the night visions, and behold, One like the Son of Man, coming with the clouds of heaven! He *came to* the Ancient of Days, and they brought Him near before Him" (Dan 7:13).

He himself declares that he leaves the world so that he may "come" to the Father: "Now I am no longer in the world, but these are in the world, and I *come* to You.... Now I *come* to You, and these things I speak in the world" (John 17:11, 13a; cp. Luke 9:51; 24:51; John 8:14; 13:1, 3; 14:28; 16:28; Acts 1:10). Thus, he comes into heaven upon his leaving the earth.

The metaphorical coming of Christ

Beyond these spiritual comings and in addition to the bodily second coming (see below), Scripture speaks of another sort of coming of Christ. This "coming" is a metaphorical coming: it is an image, a symbolic presentation of his providential wrath in *historical judgments upon men*. Let me explain.

The Old Testament frequently employs clouds as symbols of God's wrath and judgment. We often see God surrounded with foreboding clouds which express his unapproachable holiness and righteousness (Gen 15:17; Exo 13:21–22; 14:19–20; 19:9, 16–19; Deut 4:11; Job 22:14; Psa

18:8ff; 97:2; 104:3; Isa 19:1; Eze 32:7–8). In addition, Scripture poetically portrays God in certain judgment scenes as *coming in the clouds* to wreak historical vengeance upon his enemies.

One clear example of this sort of metaphorical divine coming appears in Isaiah 19. There we read: "The burden against Egypt. Behold, the LORD rides on a swift cloud, and will come into Egypt; the idols of Egypt will totter at his presence, and the heart of Egypt will melt in its midst" (Isa 19:1).[5] This occurs in the Old Testament era when the Assyrian king Esarhaddon conquers Egypt in 671 BC. Obviously it does not imply a coming of God to earth while literally riding on a cloud.

The New Testament picks up this judgment imagery and speaks metaphorically of Christ's coming in judgment clouds during history. Matthew 26:64, for instance, must speak of a first-century "coming to judge." Christ says that his accusers — the Jewish high priest and the Sanhedrin — will witness it: "Nevertheless, I say *to you*, hereafter *you* will see the Son of Man sitting at the right hand of the Power, and *coming* on the clouds of heaven" (Matt 26:64).

According to Matthew 24:30 the Jews of "this generation" (Matt 23:36; 24:34) would see a sign that the Son of Man is in heaven on the throne rather than on the earth in a tomb: "Then will appear the sign of the Son of man in heaven."[6] The sign that the Son of Man is in heaven is the smoking rubble of Jerusalem, which he prophesies beforehand (Matt 24:2, 15–21; cf. Acts 2:16–22, 36–40).

Christ teaches a parable regarding God's AD 70 judgment on Israel in Matthew 21:40. Here in the Parable of the Landowner, he presents the Jews as resisting God's will, killing the prophets, then killing God's Son (Matt 21:33–39). After presenting the parable, he asks: "Therefore, when the owner of the vineyard *comes*, what will he do to those vinedressers?" The interpretation is evident even to many premillennialists. Henry Alford, for instance, makes the following important observation:

> We may observe that our Lord makes "when the Lord cometh" *coincide with the destruction of Jerusalem,* which is incontestably the overthrow of

---

[5] 2 Sam 22:8, 10; Psa 18:7–15; 68:4, 33; 97:2–5; 104:3; Isa 13:1, 9; 26:21; 30:27; Joel 2:1, 2; Mic 1:3; Nah 1:2ff; Zep 1:4, 14–15.

[6] Alfred Marshall, *The Interlinear NASB-NIV Parallel New Testament in Greek and English* (Grand Rapids: Zondervan, 1993), 79. See also: KJV, NKJV. The Greek word order is important here. The New American Standard Bible alters that word order thus confusing the reader.

> the wicked husbandmen. This passage therefore forms an important key to our Lord's prophecies, and a decisive justification for those who like myself, firmly hold that *the coming of the Lord* is, in many places, to be identified, primarily, with that overthrow.[7]

But Scripture most definitely teaches a literal, corporeal, public coming as well. And this is called:

The literal coming of Christ

The Christian conception of history is linear, rather than cyclical. Because of this, God-governed history has a beginning — and it will have an end. The Scripture not only informs us of the world's creation, but also of its conclusion.

The universe will not endure a naturalistic heat destruction under extreme gravitational attraction, as per evolutionary mythology. Rather, it will experience a supernatural heat renovation through divine personal intervention, as per revelational theology (2 Thess 1:6–10; 2 Pet 3:7, 10–12). So then, the end will come about by the personal, sovereign intervention of the Lord Jesus Christ in great power and public glory.

A corporeal return of Christ is evident in Scripture. For instance, consider Luke's report of Christ's ascension:

> Now when He had spoken these things, while they watched, He was taken up, and a cloud received Him out of their sight. And while they looked steadfastly toward heaven as He went up, behold, two men stood by them in white apparel, who also said, "Men of Galilee, why do you stand gazing up into heaven? This same Jesus, who was taken up from you into heaven, will so come in like manner as you saw Him go into heaven." (Acts 1:9–11)

Here Luke clearly refers to the second coming. He carefully reports that the disciples are "beholding" (*bleponton*, present participle, Acts 1:9a) him as he ascends; he is received "from the eyes of them" (*apo ton ophthalmon auton*, v. 9b); they are "gazing" (*atenizontes*) as he is "going" (v. 10); they are "looking" (*blepontes*, v. 11); they "beheld" (*etheasasthe*). His ascension is most definitely a visible phenomenon involving his tangible resurrected body (Luke 24:39; John 20:27).

---

[7] Henry Alford, *Alford's Greek Testament: An Exegetical and Critical Commentary*, 5th ed. (Cambridge: University Press, 1875; Grand Rapids: Guardian, 1976), 1:216 (emph. his).

The word translated "gazing" (*atenizontes*) derives from *antenizo*, from which our term "attention" arises. It means "look intently at" (EDNT 1:177), even "stare at" (BAGD 148). As Alexander expresses it: "The Greek verb strictly denotes tension or straining of the eyes."[8]

The word *etheasasthe* derives from *theaomai*, from which we get our word "theater." The verb connotes "intensive, thorough, lingering, astonished, reflective, comprehending observation."[9] And Luke records that an actual visible cloud appears to carry the Lord away (Acts 1:9). This cloud "is probably to be interpreted as the cloud of the Shekhinah," the same cloud witnessed at the transfiguration (Matt 17:5).[10] All references to the Shekinah cloud present it as a visible phenomenon.

The angelic messengers resolutely declare that "this same Jesus" — the Jesus they knew for over three years, whom they physically "handled" (1 John 1:1; Luke 24:39; John 20:27) and who is now in a tangible resurrected body (Luke 24:39–40; John 20:27) — will "so come *in like manner* [*on tropon*] as you saw Him go into heaven" (Acts 1:11). The Greek *on tropon* literally means "what manner." The Greek phrase "never indicates mere certainty or vague resemblance; but wherever it occurs in the New Testament, denotes identity of mode or manner"[11] (e.g., Acts 7:28; 2 Tim 3:8). Consequently, we have express biblical warrant to expect a visible, bodily, glorious return of Christ paralleling in kind his leaving this earth at his ascension. This glorious event is mentioned in a number of Scripture passages.[12]

Consequently, just as the beginning of history involves Christ (John 1:3; Col 1:16), so will its end (1 Cor 15:23–24). He is the "Alpha and the Omega, the Beginning and the End" (Rev 1:8; cf. 3:14; 21:6; 22:13). The Lord will return in great power and much glory in our future.

---

[8] Joseph A. Alexander, *The Acts of the Apostles Explained* (New York: Anson D. F. Randolph, 1857), 1: 1:14.

[9] *EDNT* 2:136.

[10] F. F. Bruce, *The Book of Acts* (NICNT) (2d. ed.: Grand Rapids: Eerdmans, 1988), 41. A.M. Ramsey,"What was the Ascension?" *Studiorum Novi Testamenti Societas*. Bulletin II (Oxford, 1951): 43ff. See: Exo 16:10; 19:16; 24:15; 40:34–38; Matt 17:5.

[11] Alexander, *Acts*, 1:16.

[12] For example, to list but a few: Matt 13:30, 39–43; 24:36–25:56; 1Cor 11:26; 15:23–24, 51–52; Phil 3:20–21; Col 3:4; 1 Thess 4:13–17; Tit 2:13; Rev 20:9.

Preterism and Prophecy

As mentioned previously, all Christians — even dispensational futurists — are also preterists to some extent. And necessarily so. This is due to Christians recognizing Christ's fulfilling a great many of the Old Testament Messianic prophecies at his first coming.[13]

On these points, Christians differ from the "futurism" of Orthodox Judaism. Orthodox Jews in antiquity and still today insist that Christians are misapplying the Old Testament's Messianic prophecies to past events.[14] They hold that in the future "when Israel fully accepts God's rule, then the messiah will come."[15] Glasson notes: "Orthodox Jews at the present time look for a Messiah who will reign on earth for a limited period. This has been Jewish teaching for many centuries and goes back to pre-Christian times. We have evidence from the BC period in 1 Enoch 91–108."[16] Ancient rabbinic Judaism believes that "the messianic era could not come before Elijah had set things straight."[17]

In fact, "the belief in the [future] coming of the Messiah is one of the 'Thirteen Articles of Creed' of Maimonides included in the daily Jewish ritual."[18] Thus, "in our day many Jews still await the coming of the true Messiah 'in the End of Days.'"[19] Of the incarnation as revealed in prophecy, early church father Athanasius (AD 296–373) writes: "So the Jews

---

[13] See the list of passages in *PEBP* 219–23.

[14] See for instance: Justin Martyr, *Dialogue with Trypho the Jew* in *ANF* v. 1. For example, regarding Isa 7:14 Trypho challenges Justin (chs 77ff): "Proceed then to make this plain to us, that we may see how you prove that that [passage] refers to this Christ of yours. For we assert that the prophecy relates to Hezekiah" (237). For some helpful insights, see: D. S. Russell, *From Early Judaism to Early Church* (Philadelphia: Fortress, 1986) and Geza Vermes, *Jesus and the World of Judaism* (Philadelphia: Fortress, 1983).

[15] *DJBP* 426.

[16] T. Francis Glasson, "The Temporary Messianic Kingdom and the Kingdom of God." *Journal of the Theological Studies* 41:2 (1990). 517.

[17] Jacob Neusner, *First-Century Judaism in Crisis: Yohanan ben Zakkai and the Renaissance of Torah* (Eugene, Ore.: Wipf & Stock, 2000 [rep. 1975]),15.

[18] David Bridger, ed., *The New Jewish Encyclopedia* (New York: Behrman, 1976), 317. Moses Maimonides (1135– 1204) was the greatest codifier of Judaism in the Middle Ages.

[19] David Bridger, ed., *The New Jewish Encyclopedia* (New York: Behrman, 1976), 318.

are trifling, and the time in question, which they refer to the future, is actually come."[20]

The orthodox preterist approach holds, for instance, that all of the first portion of the Olivet Discourse (Matt 24:1–34//) is fulfilled in events leading up to and entering into the Jewish War in AD 67–70.[21] And in the Book of Revelation almost all of John's prophecies are also fulfilled in the fall of Jerusalem (AD 70).[22] Orthodox preterists have strong exegetical indicators undergirding our system, which I will briefly illustrate. But I must first quickly mention two basic principles involved in the preterist hermeneutic.

Two foundational principles for sound biblical hermeneutics are: (1) The clearer (didactic discourse) statements of Scripture interpret the less clear (figurative imagery); and (2) Scripture interprets Scripture. With these principles in mind, I will quickly illustrate the preterist argument from the Olivet Discourse and Revelation. I contend that rival perspectives breach both principles.

The Olivet Discourse

That Matthew 24:4–33 speaks of Jerusalem's destruction is both eminently reasonable and exegetically necessary. Even futurists must admit to *some* preteristic elements in the Discourse. Dispensationalists such as Paul Enns, Tim LaHaye, Louis A. Barbieri, John F. Walvoord, Thomas D. Ice, and others generally hold this regarding Matthew 24:1–2. For instance, Enns writes: "these words found their fulfillment in A.D. 70 when Titus destroyed Jerusalem."[23]

Amillennialists, such as Robert L Reymond, Kim Riddlebarger, and Cornelis P. Venema, postmillennialists, such as John J. Davis, David Chi-

---

[20] Athanasius, *Incarnation* 40:1. Cf. Pinches Lapide, Pinches and U. Luz, *Jesus in Two Perspectives: A Jewish-Christian Dialog* (Minneapolis: Augsburg, 1985).

[21] See ch 5 below for the full rationale for dividing the chapter at 24:36.

[22] See: Kenneth L. Gentry, Jr., in C. Marvin Pate, *Four Views of the Book of Revelation*. David Chilton, *The Days of Vengeance: An Exposition of the Book of Revelation* (Fort Worth: Dominion, 1987). Douglas Kelly, *Revelation* (Cornwall, Eng.: Mentor, 2012).

[23] Paul P. Enns, in *DPT*, 286. See also: Thomas Ice in *PEBP* 249. LaHaye, *PSB* 1152. Pentecost, *Thy Kingdom Come* (Wheaton: Victory, 1990), 249. Warren W. Wiersbe, *Bible Exposition Commentary* (Wheaton, Ill.: Victor, 1989), 2:86. Walvoord, *PKH* 381. Louis A. Barbieri, Jr., "Matthew," *BKC*, 2:76.

lton, Greg L. Bahnsen, and Keith L. Mathison, as well as premillennialists, such as George E. Ladd and Wayne Grudem, hold that the fuller passage presents both the AD 70 event and the second advent to which it points.[24] Historic premillennialists do the same. For instance, Sung Wook Chung states: "For Jesus, then, 'great tribulation' refers neither to the events of the second century BC nor to a period of time only just preceding his return but, at least in part, to the distress at the time of the destruction of Jerusalem, the burning of the city, and the razing of the temple by the Romans in AD 70."[25]

That Matthew 24:2–33 (excluding v. 27[26]) is already fulfilled seems quite obvious on the two following bases.

First, its introductory *context* strongly suggests it. In Matthew 23 Jesus sorely rebukes the "scribes and Pharisees" *of his own day* (Matt 23:2ff). He urges *them* finally to "fill up then the measure of your fathers" who killed the prophets (23:31–32).[27] He says that they are a "generation" of vipers (23:33) that will persecute and slay his disciples (23:34). He notes that upon *them* will come all the righteous blood shed on the earth (23:35). He

---

[24] Robert Reymond, *A New Systematic Theology of the Christian Faith.* Nashville: Thomas Nelson, 1998), 999–1008. Kim Riddlebarger, *A Case for Amillennialism: Understanding the End Times.* Grand Rapids: Baker, ch 13. Venema, *The Promise of the Future* (Edinburgh: Banner of Truth, 2000), 142–158. John J. Davis, *The Victory of Christ's Kingdom* (Moscow, Ida.: Canon, 1996; rep. 1986), 107. David Chilton *Productive Christians in an Age of Guilt Manipulators* (3rd ed.; Tyler, Tex.: Institute for Christian Economics, 1985), *passim.* Greg L. Bahnsen, *Victory in Jesus: The Bright Hope of Postmillennialism* (Texarkana, Ark.: CMP, 1999), 12–17. Keith L. Mathison, *Postmillennialism: An Eschatology of Hope* (Phillipsburg, N.J.: Presbyterian and Reformed, 1999), 111–15. Wayne Grudem, *Systematic Theology: An Introduction to Biblical Doctrine* (Grand Rapids: Zondervan, 1994). George E. Ladd, *The Presence of the Future* (Grand Rapids: Eerdmans, 1974), 310–11. Unfortunately, Bahnsen's argument is marred by whoever transcribed it after his death.

[25] Sung Wook Chung in Craig L. Blomberg and Sung Wook Chung, eds. *A Case for Historic Premillennialism: An Alternative to "Left Behind" Eschatology (*Grand Rapids: Baker, 2009), 73.

[26] Verse 27 mentions the second coming — but only to distinguish it from the metaphorical coming in AD 70 of which the Lord is speaking in this section of the Discourse.

[27] As did John Baptist before him (Matt 3:1–12).

then dogmatically asserts: "Truly I say unto you, all these things shall come upon *this generation*" (23:36).

In Matthew 23:37–24:2 Jesus weeps over Jerusalem (Matt 23:37–38) then declares that its temple will be destroyed stone-by-stone (Matt 24:2) — all to the disciples' great surprise and dismay (Matt 24:3). Regarding these actions and statements the disciples ask, "When shall these things be?" As a matter of historical record we know the temple was totally dismantled and destroyed in August, AD 70: "Since that time [AD 70], the Temple has never been rebuilt, though the remains of its foundation walls are an archaeological highlight of modern Jerusalem."[28]

Second, its express temporal indicators demand it. We must not miss the clear references to Christ's *contemporary expectation*. Enclosing the discourse's relevant portion, we have the Lord's own time designation. Leading up to the Matthew 24 the Lord dogmatically asserts in Matthew 23:36: "*all* these things shall come upon *this* generation." Then after concluding that portion of his prophecy, he repeats the time frame: "Truly I say unto you, *this* generation shall not pass, till all these things be fulfilled" (Matt 24:34). Contextually the "this generation" of Matthew 24:34 *must* involve the same time frame as that in Matthew 23:36.

In fact, Matthew 24:34 solemnly affirms the matter. The Lord is dramatically emphasizing a point when he begins a statement with: "truly" (the Greek word is the familiar *amen*, which means "so be it"). Thus, here he powerfully draws the disciples' attention to what he is about to say — just as he does in 24:2, when he makes the statement spurring the whole Discourse. In fact, he does not simply declare this with an *amen* ("truly"); he underscores what he is about to say with an additional attention-getting: "I tell you."

Furthermore, a direct-literal translation of the Greek reads: "Truly I tell you that by no means passes away generation this until all these things happens."[29] The "by no means" is a strong, double negative (*ou me*). Jesus places it early in his statement for added emphasis. He is staking his credibility, as it were, on his prophecy's absolute certainty.[30]

---

[28] Neusner, *DJBP* 626. Unfortunately, "archaeological remains" of the temple "are rather small" (625).

[29] Marshall, *Interlinear NASB-NIV*, 80.

[30] He contrasts the durability and integrity of his prophetic word here with that of the material universe in Matt 24:35: "Heaven and earth will pass away, but My words will not pass away."

But what does Jesus so carefully and emphatically declare to them? Whatever the symbolic imagery in some of the preceding verses may indicate (e.g., Matt 24:29–31), Jesus clearly states that "all these things [*panta tauta*]" will occur *before* "this generation" passes away. We also find the phrase "this generation" in Matthew 11:16; 12:39-45; and 23:36. Only with great difficulty may these references mean anything other than Jesus' contemporary generation.

Even dispensationalist Thomas Ice admits: "It is true that every other use of 'this generation' in Matthew ... refers to Christ's contemporaries."[31] But then he denies that this one instance does so! We must understand that "most biblical writers seem to consider thirty to forty years to be a normal generation (Deut 2:14; Job 42:16; Psa 95:10).

After presenting the coming destruction of the temple, the Lord segues into the second advent. The historical judgment at AD 70 is an early warning indicator of the greater (final!) judgment to come at Christ's return. He employs the near demonstrative regarding the events tied to Matthew 24:2–34: these events will come during "*this* [*tauta*] generation" (Matt 24:34). He uses the far demonstrative in 24:36 to point to the second advent involving "*that* [*ekeines*] day." Thus, the "great tribulation" (24:21) is coming *soon* — upon "this generation" (23:36; 24:34; cf. 1 Thess 2:16) — with certain signs foreshadowing it (24:4–8). But the second advent (which he deals with in Matt 24:36ff) awaits "that" far away day and hour.[32]

Preterism has a secure foundation in Matthew 24:3–34. Indeed, many early church fathers recognized this.[33]

The Book of Revelation

Surprisingly to most evangelicals, the judgments in Revelation 4–19 lie in our past. We may discern this from John's various time indicators. And quite significantly, these time-statements appear in his less symbolic,

---

[31] Thomas D. Ice in Ice and Kenneth L Gentry, Jr. *The Great Tribulation: Past or Future?* (Grand Rapids: Kregel, 1999), 103.

[32] For a listing of exegetical reasons for seeing a division of the time and events between Matt 24:34 and Matt 24:36, see later ch 5 below.

[33] See especially Eusebius, *Ecclesiastical History* 3:7:1–2; *The Clementine Homilies* 3:15; and Cyprian, *Treatises* 12:1:6, 15. For more detail, see: Gary DeMar and Francis X. Gumerlock. *The Early Church and the End of the World*. Powder Springs (Geo.: American Vision, 2006).

more didactic introduction and conclusion, before and after the symbolic visions of seven-headed beasts, lion-headed locusts, and so forth.

As we begin a brief consideration of this, we should note that Revelation closely relates to the Olivet Discourse (both the Matt 24 and Luke 21 versions), as most interpreters recognize. We may discern this from the following evidence:

1. Both expect the events to occur soon (Matt 24:34; Rev 1:1, 3).
2. Both uniquely merge Daniel 7:13 and Zechariah 12:10 (Matt 24:30; Rev 1:7). Revelation 1:7 is the theme of Revelation; Matthew 24:30 is the goal of this portion of the discourse.
3. Both refer to "the great tribulation" (Matt 24:21; Rev 7:14).
4. The first four seals in Revelation 6:1–8 follow the order of and summarize the flow of events in Matthew 24:4ff: wars, international strife, famines, earthquakes, persecution, and eclipses of the sun and moon, along with falling stars.
5. Revelation cites Jesus' words regarding the temple's destruction (Luke 21:24; Rev 11:2) and his statement about the righteous blood shed on the earth (Matt 23:35; Rev 18:24).

There is more evidence for John's Revelation effectively being a symbolic re-working of Jesus' Discourse. But these should suffice for my present purpose. It should not surprise us, then, that the orthodox preterist argument is as clear and compelling in Revelation as it is in Matthew 24.

Revelation 1:1 opens Revelation's prophecies and prepares the reader for them: "The Revelation of Jesus Christ, which God gave unto him, to shew unto his servants things which must *shortly* [*en tachei*] come to pass." John reiterates this by employing synonymous terminology in Revelation 1:3c where we read his clear statement: "the time is at hand" (*kairos engus*).

John again repeats these expectations as he closes: "And he said to me, 'These words are faithful and true'; and the Lord, the God of the spirits of the prophets, sent His angel to show to His bond-servants the things which *must shortly be done*" (*genesthai en tachei*) (Rev 22:6). "And he said to me, 'Do not seal up the words of the prophecy of this book, *for the time is near* [*ho kairos gar engus estin*]" (22:10). The point should be clear to the original recipient: John expects the events he prophesies to occur soon.

Evangelicals cannot lightly dismiss these book-bracketing, temporal indicators in Revelation, such is the evangelical commitment to the integrity and veracity of God's word. Evangelicals firmly believe that they must "let God be found true" (Rom 3:4) and that "the Scriptures cannot be broken" (John 10:35). Furthermore, John is writing to seven historical churches (Rev 1:4, 11; 2:1–3:22; 22:16), which are experiencing and expecting even more trouble (2:1–3:22). He is currently sharing with those in "tribulation" (1:9), who have witnessed loved ones killed for their faith (2:13) and who are expecting prison (2:10). He expects those very churches to hear (1:3; 22:10) the "revelation [i.e., uncovering of truth]" (1:1) and to heed the things in it (1:3; 22:7). And the reason they must do so is because: the events are *near* (1:1, 3; 22:6, 10).

The agonizing cries from John's fellow sufferers receives special emphasis. In Revelation 6 the martyrs in heaven plead for God's righteous vindication: "They cried with a loud voice, saying, 'How long, O Lord, holy and true, until You judge and avenge our blood on those who dwell on the earth?" They receive heavenly comfort in that "a white robe was given to each of them; and it was said to them that they should rest *a little while longer*" (6:10–11).

Original relevance, then, is the lock and the time-texts the key for opening Revelation's heavy door. What clearer terms for contemporary expectation could John use other than those he employs in Revelation 1:1, 3; 22:6, 10 and other places?

Final Observations

Some evangelicals like to point out that a Roman Catholic priest Luis De Alcazar (1554–1613) presents the first formal, full-scale preterist approach to Revelation. Unfortunately, this is an example of the "genetic fallacy" in argumentation. This interpretive fallacy discounts something because of its early use by an unpopular group rather than on its own merits.

Furthermore, this complaint overlooks two countervailing facts: (1) Preteristic tendencies can be found well before Alcazar among the early church fathers in a number of passages, including Matthew 24 (e.g., Eusebius, *Eccl. Hist*. 3:7) and Revelation (e.g., Andreas of Cappadocia's commentary on Revelation). Alcazar simply presents a more consistent, full-scale preterist interpretation of Revelation. (2) They tend to overlook the fact that the futurist system itself is also highly developed by another Jesuit priest from the same era. Ice writes: "Jesuit Francisco Ribera (1537–1591) was one of the first to revive an undeveloped form of futurism around 1580."[34] Thus, the same "problem" of Roman Catholic involvement is true with a formal, full-scale *futurist* approach to Revelat-ion.

As with any system developed by sinful men and held in fallen minds, we must recognize that no one hermeneutic approach can be always followed. Consider the "futurism" of dispensationalism, for instance. No dispensationalist is "pure" futurist. He believes *some* prophecies of Scripture have already occurred, and therefore must be interpreted preteristically. After all, Isaiah 7:14 prophesies the virgin birth of Christ. This is a past event in our day; which we cannot interpret futuristically. As noted previously we could mention any number of other passages dealing with the coming of the Messiah in the first century.

Significantly, preterism has a sound basis in New Testament theology, textual exegesis, and historical analysis as we have seen in both the Olivet Discourse and Revelation. Consequently, we should not discount a preterist approach to Revelation, for instance, as rendering Revelation irrelevant today, as some do. Shall we declare that the many Old Testament prophecies concerning the coming of Christ to be "irrelevant" because they involve historical matters already occurring in our past? Are we to set aside historical references to Christ in the Gospels and the Apostles in Acts, simply because they are dealing with "ancient history"? Surely not.

We must also remember that almost all of the New Testament epistles are what we call "occasional epistles." That is, they are dealing with specific occasions regarding the historical experiences of the first-century Christians. For instance, 1 Corinthians deals with a great many particular sins in a local church in Greece 2000 years ago. Is it therefore irrelevant to us today?

The Epistle to the Hebrews warns first-century Jewish converts to Christianity that it is both dangerous and pointless to return to temple-based Judaism because the temple system is "about to disappear" (Heb 8:13). Of course, from our perspective the temple system disappeared

---

[34]Thomas D. Ice in Ice and Timothy Demy. *When the Trumpet Sounds* (Eugene, Ore.: Harvest, 199), 16. He confesses this just two pages after citing Merrill C. Tenney's statement that "the first systematic presentation of the preterist viewpoint originated in the early seventeenth century with Alcazar, a Jesuit friar" (14). Premillennialist Chung also recognizes this derivation of futurism: Chung in Blomberg and Chung, *Historic Premillennialism*, 9.

long ago. Indeed, the writer sends this glorious epistle to "Hebrews." Is it irrelevant to those of us who are Gentiles and who live centuries after the demise of the temple system?

We should understand several very important "relevancies" of fulfilled prophecies such as in Revelation: (1) They demonstrate the general truth that God's prophetic word will come to pass. After all, in several places we already see a past fulfillment. Thus, when we read such passages, they affirm the truthfulness of God's word.

(2) Though Revelation prophesies events that occur almost 2000 years ago, we can learn *principles* of God's operations in history from those events. We see God protecting his people, judging his enemies, leaving a witness for the ongoing church, demonstrating the catastrophic results of rebellion against God by those who are his people, and more. Thus, we may discern ethical and spiritual lessons through those first-century trials of faith.

(3) Since Revelation largely speaks of events occurring in and around AD 70, we have an inspired interpretation about what becomes of the temple and old covenant Judaism, both of which were central to redemptive history for so many centuries. We see that God overthrows the temple and judges Israel in order to bring his new covenant promises upon an enlarged people of God, no longer tying his covenant to a particular race, a specific land, a single temple, and ritualistic worship. Thus, preterists believe with Paul that old, fulfilled, historic Scriptures are "written for our admonition" (1 Cor 10:11).

But now we are ready to introduce the doctrinal aberrations of:

Hyper-preterism

Hyper-preterism (or Full Preterism or Consistent Preterism), is an extension of preterism. But it is an extension that has pushed its innovative theology beyond biblical limits.

I will survey in a summary fashion just ten areas of concern regarding current Hyper-Preterist theology. This brief survey will highlight theological matters that are not minor issues of adiaphora[35] in a narrow field.

---

[35] "Adiaphora" is from the Greek word that means "indifferent things." In Christian theology it refers to things that are indifferent, i.e., positions that are tolerable among believers. They are neither commanded or forbidden in Scripture statements or principles.

By departing from historic Christianity in these areas Hyper-preterism is constructing a new, aberrant theology; it is radically reworking the Christian doctrinal system. And this is only the beginning. Some of the issues listed below are not directly matters of creedal formulation, but are nevertheless evidences of dangerous tampering with the structure of Christian theology.

The second advent of Christ

The *raison d'etre* of Hyper-preterism is the denial of the future, public, bodily, glorious return of Christ. Hyper-preterist spokesman Ed Stevens clearly affirms: "Christ returned in AD 70!" (WH 5). He complains about the failure of the creeds in this regard: "The creeds reflect that same futurist perspective seemingly [!] unaware the events had occurred in 70 AD" (CPO). Ward Fenley has written a book titled: *The Second Coming of Jesus Christ Already Happened.*[36] A website supporting this view is titled: "PreteristCentral.com: Affirming Christ's Second Coming Fulfilled." Hence, the title of this book: *Have We Missed the Second Coming?*

The resurrection of the dead

Stevens states that "the resurrection and judgment at AD 70 were once-for-all events" (WH, 33). He explains that "full preterists believe the Bible teaches that a collective resurrection would occur. We just [!] disagree with traditional 'interpretations and applications' of the TIME and NATURE of that resurrection" (RGA).[37] He cautions his followers: "No Christian should jump for joy as we realize how mistaken the early church was in their understanding of the time and nature of eschatological fulfill-

---

[36] Ward Fenley, *The Second Coming of Jesus Christ Already Happened* (Sacramento: Kingdom of Sovereign Grace, 1997). See also: Charles S. Meek, *Christian Hope through Fulfilled Prophecy: Is Your Church Teaching Error about the Last Days and Second Coming?* (Faith Facts, 2013). Don K. Preston, *AD 70: A Shadow of the "Real" End?* (JaDon, 2013).

[37] Whereas Stevens cavalierly suggests he "just" disagrees with the nature and timing of these events, Preston admits that "this would require a radical alteration of our concept of the judgement and the resurrection. While it is true that it requires such an alteration, the change brings us in tune with the Bible and this is never wrong." Don K. Preston, *2 Peter 3: The Late Great Kingdom* (Shawnee, Okla.: n. p., 1990), 13. Stevens' "just" disagreeing with the nature and timing of the second advent is like a Mormon declaring: "We just disagree with the nature of God and his eternality."

ments. But, we shouldn't hesitate too long in admitting their failure and correcting them" (RGA).

The resurrection body

Regarding the resurrection body, Stevens argues that it will be "raised immortal with a spiritual body like Christ's" (RGA). This is because "Christ's kingdom is not of this physical realm. It is a spiritual kingdom. It requires a spiritual resurrection to get there, not a physical resuscitation" (RGA). He even tags his view to a controversial theologian[38]: "I believe most full preterists would agree with that. Murray Harris, in his two books, *Raised Immortal* and *From Grave To Glory*" (RGA). Thus, according to Stevens, "the real question that must be addressed is whether the Bible (not the creeds) allows ... 'any other type of resurrection than a bodily one.' Just because the creeds may not allow it, does not mean the Bible does not allow it" (RGA).

The final judgment

Stevens argues that "the resurrection and judgment at AD 70 were once-for-all events like the Cross and Christ's resurrection. They are never to be repeated" (WH, 33). Thus, creedal theology is inherently mistaken: "even though no particular view of eschatology was defined, there is a definite future slant to creedal eschatology statements. The NT teaches a *future* resurrection, judgment, coming and end because those events hadn't happened before it was written" (CPO). Consequently, "the wording of the creeds could be amended to indicate that they are merely reflecting the NT's original futurist perspective, but not necessarily imposing a futurist approach upon anyone after the first century" (CPO).

---

[38] See for instance: "Trinity Prof Attacked for Resurrection Teaching," *Christianity Today*, 36:13 (Nov. 9, 1992): 62; "The Mother of All Muddles," *Christianity Today*, 37:3 (Apr. 5, 1993): 62-66; Gary R. Habermas, "The Recent Evangelical Debate On The Bodily Resurrection Of Jesus: A Review Article" and Francis J. Beckwith, "Identity and Resurrection — A Review Article" in *Journal of the Evangelical Theological Society*, 33:3 (Sept., 1990): 370-81. Harris — and the Hyper-preterists — need to read the works of Geerhardus Vos and Herman Ridderbos in order to understand the physical resurrection in light of Paul's argument in 1 Cor 15.

The consummation

Most Hyper-Preterists teach that the earth will last forever. This is the major theme of the Noe book, *Beyond the End Times*, for which Stevens writes the Foreword (BET). To the historic Christian teaching regarding the end of the world, Noe responds: "The Bible never speaks of an end of time" (BET, 91). "It won't ever end" (BET, 265). And just to be sure, he writes: "The world is never, repeat never-ever going to end. We live an a never-ending world" (BET, 45). Stevens' Foreword laments in this regard: "For too long we have been stymied by eschatological views that have not been developed beyond 2nd-century concepts" (BET, x).

The Holy Spirit's work

Though not directly a creedal issue, Stevens' radical alteration of eschatology changes the role of the Holy Spirit in redemption. Here we are beginning to see some of the systemic problems generated out of Hyper-preterism in the important realm of soteriology: "His role as Paraclete has come to an end.... We now have Christ Himself indwelling our hearts" (WICW). "So even though we may not have the Spirit indwelling and empowering us today, we have something better" (WICW).

The Trinity

Stevens is so concerned about creedal theology that he makes dangerous suggestions regarding the historic formulation of the doctrine of the Trinity: "I think the creeds might have gone too far in trying to define the Divine Nature in ways the Scripture does not necessarily dictate. What if the creeds formulated an interpretive position on the 'Trinity' that is unbiblical.... If we had just stuck with the statements of Scripture ... the Jewish people and many other might have been better able to accept Christ" [perhaps like they did in the book of Acts? — KLG] (WICW). In this regard, we should note that some of Stevens' followers have even become Unitarians, as he himself well knows from a controversy that shook his own Hyper-preterist ministry.[39]

---

[39] Edward E. Stevens, "Wanda Shirk & PIE," *Kingdom Counsel* (April 1994-Sept. 1996): 3-17.

The doctrine of hell

Some Hyper-preterists have begun noticing the similarity of Jerusalem destruction language and the biblical warnings regarding Hell. Consequently, they are applying the biblical teaching regarding Hell to the events of AD 70. Samuel Dawson writes: "If hell is what Jesus said it was, *hell is not a place, but an event* — the unstoppable fiery destruction of Jerusalem in 70 A.D."[40] This serves well as another illustration of and warning about their exegetical naivete.

The role of Satan

Some Hyper-preterists teach the current death of Satan. A contributor to Stevens' Hyper-preterist website, David A. Green, writes: "The term preterism in this article refers to the belief that all (or virtually all) Bible prophecy is fulfilled. It does not refer to the belief of partial preterism, which says that the Great Tribulation is fully past but that a great many other things are not fulfilled, most importantly: the Second Coming, the death of the Devil, the general Resurrection of the dead, and the Great White Throne Judgment" (PEC, fn 1). Don Preston writes in an e-mail posted March 26, 2002 on the "PlanetPreterist" website: "Jesus has indeed cast Satan into hell and broken his power;" and "Satan has been finally defeated, cast into hell."

The gospel of Christ

As Hyper-preterism continues through mutation and cell division, even the Gospel of salvation is theoretically open for re-interpretation. Green, on Stevens' website, admits: "Some preterists and others have said that since the creeds were written by, and have been endorsed by, the 'institutional church,' (meaning potentially, the false church) there is no reason to presume that the true Gospel ever found its way into the creeds" (PEC, fn 2). Though he does not agree with these concerns, he has to fend against insiders in the movement who do.

---

[40] Samuel G. Dawson, *Jesus' Teaching on Hell: A Place or an Event?* (Puyallup, Wash.: Gospel Themes, 1997). His website advertises his study on Hell: "after years of study, he discovered that none of our traditional concepts of hell can be found in the teaching of Jesus Christ!"

Conclusion

Stevens muses: "I am surprised at Gentry's hesitancy to believe the historic Church could have missed a few things" (RGA). A "few things"? Hyper-preterism, untethered from the anchor of historic Christianity, is being blown about by every wind of doctrine. The Hyper-preterist will not be able to stop the destructive winds by arbitrarily crying out on his own recognizance: "Peace! Be still!" We will increasingly witness how Hymanean shipwrecks will litter the Hyper-preterist shores wherever its waters may flow.

McGrath aptly warns about heresy in general: "Heresy is thus clearly seen to be a defective version of Christianity. It is a version of Christianity, in the sense that it accepts the major premises of faith — which distinguishes it from unbelief, or non-Christian beliefs. But precisely because it is inadequate, it poses a threat to Christianity.... Heresy is simply second rate Christianity."[41] And, as I will show, Hyper-preterism is heresy.

---

[41] Alistair E. McGrath, *Studies in Doctrine* (Grand Rapids: Zondervan, 1997), 309.

Chapter 2

THE HYPER-PRETERIST ERRORS SUMMARIZED

Introduction

As I indicated in chapter 1, preterism properly understood — *orthodox* preterism — is basically a hermeneutical tool. It should not be pressed into service as a whole new theology, as in Hyper-preterism. It helps us understand the several New Testament prophecies regarding the destruction of the temple and Jerusalem in AD 70.

Orthodox preterists gladly accept the basic doctrines of universal Christian theology, which teach that other important biblical prophecies are not yet fulfilled. Among those unfulfilled prophecies are:

- the visible, glorious, personal second coming of Christ
- the physical resurrection of the dead
- the final corporate judgment of all men on Judgment Day
- the end of the present earth and temporal history
- the establishment of the consummate, physical new creation

Consequently, orthodox preterists affirm the basic doctrinal construct which is the universal, historic, formal, corporate, public, systematic belief of the institutional Christian church of all times.

Preterism has long been accepted as an approach to select passages of Scripture, dating all the way back to at least as early as Eusebius (AD 260–340[1]). Dispensationalist Thomas Ice admits: "There is early preterism in people like Eusebius. In fact, his work *The Proof of the Gospel* is full of preterism in relationship to the Olivet Discourse."[2]

Preterism was an especially well-known interpretive approach in the 1800s and early 1900s, though until recently "preterism" never described an entire theology. It only served to provide select hermeneutic insights

---

[1] For example, note what Eusebius declares: "Such was the reward of the iniquity of the Jews and their impiety against the Christ of God, but it is worth appending to it the infallible forecast of our Saviour in which he prophetically expounded these very things" (*Eccl. Hist.* 3:7:1). Then he begins interweaving the Olivet Discourse with Josephus' *Jewish War*.

[2] Ice, "Update on Pre-Darby Rapture Statements," audio tape. Cited in Gary DeMar and Francis X. Gumerlock, *The Early Church and the End of the World* (Powder Springs, Geo.: American Vision, 2006), 15.

into specific prophetic pronouncements limited by near-term temporal indicators.

Unfortunately, growing up out of this perspective, some over zealous interpreters have transformed this important hermeneutic device into a full-scale theological construct, creating a whole new, free-standing theology. For all practical purposes we may state that this extreme form of preterism arose as a movement in the early 1980s, though we discover a few of its distinctives a century earlier, especially in J. Stuart Russell's, *The Parousia* (1878).[3]

At the most basic level, Hyper-preterists believe that AD 70 witnesses the final accomplishment of *all* prophecies not fulfilled before that time. This includes the second advent, the resurrection of the dead, the final judgment, the consummational new heavens and new earth, and several other doctrines. A key verse in their system is Luke 21:22, which all (even dispensationalists) agree refers to AD 70: "these are days of vengeance, in order that all things which are written may be fulfilled." I will return to this verse shortly (and focus on it in detail in ch 3).

This modern movement arose largely from among members of the Stone-Campbell Restoration Movement, known as the Church of Christ (e. g., Foy E. Wallace, Jack Scott, Jesse Mills, Gene Fadely, Max King, Tim King, Don Preston, Ed Stevens, Tom Kloske, and Kurt Simmons). According to Stevens, one of its leading proponents, some "Hyper-preterists" have even become Unitarians.[4] Others are beginning to apply the biblical references to hell to the events of AD 70, thereby denying the doctrine of eternal punishment.[5]

Thus, the theological implications of the movement appear to be continually mutating. Of course, we might expect this in a movement that has no creedal moorings (as we shall see in detail in ch 6). This problem is exacerbated by the fact that it is adrift on a sea of theologically untrained

---

[3] Slightly earlier, though, a convert of Charles Finney began promoting the view that the second coming occurred in AD 70: John Humphrey Noyes (1811–86). He was the Utopian socialist, who founded the Oneida Community in 1848. He exercised little influence among orthodox Christians. See: J. D. Douglas, *Who's Who in Christian History* (Wheaton: Tyndale, 1992), 515.

[4] Ed Stevens, "Wanda Shirk & PIE," *Kingdom Counsel* (April 1994-Sept. 1996): 3–17.

[5] Samuel G. Dawson, *Jesus' Teaching on Hell: A Place or an Event?* (Puyallup, Wash.: Gospel Themes, 1997).

writers. The Foreword to a book by John Noe from this movement inadvertently highlights the (all too typical) problem: "John is not a professional theologian. He has had no formal seminary training, but that may be an advantage." Then again, lacking training in biblical languages, exegetical principles, systematic theology, and historical theology may not be as helpful as Hyper-preterists think.

Whereas orthodox preterism is a *hermeneutic* approach to specific New Testament prophecies, Hyper-preterism is more than that. It uses the specific near-term passages as a starting point for developing an entire *theology* that contradicts universal, historic Christian orthodoxy. Thus, orthodox preterism is *exegetical preterism*, working from *interpretive conclusions* drawn from New Testament prophecies regarding specific first-century events. Whereas Hyper-preterism is *theological preterism*, building on *theological implications* drawn from those select biblical texts and then read back over *all* eschatological passages.

Opponents of *any* large scale preterist analysis, especially those holding to classic dispensationalism, too easily confuse preterism and Hyper-preterism. And even when they are not actually confused over the issues, they either mention Hyper-preterism alongside of preterism (in order to discredit the orthodox version through guilt-by-association) or they stumble when trying to present the issues.

By way of example regarding their tendency to confuse the issues, evangelical theologian Norm Geisler writes: "*Extreme (full) preterism* maintains that *all* New Testament predictions are past, including those about the resurrection and the Second Coming, which likewise occurred in the first century. This model has been held by David Chilton (1951–1997) — see *Paradise Restore* and *Days of Vengeance*) and Kenneth Gentry (b. 1953 — see *Before Jerusalem Fell*)."[6] Neither Chilton nor I present Hyper-preterist doctrines in the works Geisler cites.

Thomas Ice fumbles his critique of preterism in the *Popular Encyclopedia of Bible Prophecy*. Even though he is well aware of my writings (frequently citing them), Ice states: "Preterists such as Kenneth Gentry (pp. 86–89) believe that current history is identified as the new heavens and new earth of Revelation 21–22 and 2 Peter 3:10–13."[7]

---

[6] Norman Geisler, *Systematic Theology: Church, Last Things* (Minneapolis: Bethany, 2005), 615. Emph. his. I might note that he also states the wrong date for my birth.

[7] Ice, "Preterism," in *PEBP*, 284–89.

But in the very pages that Ice cites (from my contribution to *Four Views on the Book of Revelation*), I state the *opposite* of what he reports. I write regarding the new creation in Revelation 21–22: "The new creation language suggests a first-century setting. The new creation begins flowing into history before the final consummation (which will establish a wholly new physical order, 2 Peter 3:10–13)." Thus, I believe that the 2 Peter 3 reference does *not* refer to the present spiritual new creation (as per 2 Cor 5:17; Gal 6:15), but points to the final, permanent new creation order established only at the end of history. The present spiritual new creation in Christ *anticipates* the consummate new creation at the end of history, but it does not fully embody it.

A few sentences later, after specifically mentioning only my name ---- when stating "preterists such as Kenneth Gentry" — Ice confusedly declares: "Because of the current spread of preterism, pastors and teachers need to be prepared to defend *orthodox eschatology* from this attack. Those who *believe that Christ came in AD 70* will be found looking for our Lord's any-moment return when He does rapture the church without any signs or warning."[8]

Note that Ice here lumps all preterism into the Hyper-preterist camp and writes-off preterism as opposed to "orthodox eschatology." This practice is as unconscionable as it is unending. Such errors and mis-statements are unfortunate in that orthodox preterists oppose Hyper-preterism just as vigorously as do dispensationalists. We understand that Hyper-preterism strikes at the fundamentals of the faith.

Unfortunately, even historic premillennialists can stumble here, too. Blomberg and Chung state that:

> "preterism has taken on a higher profile in some Reformed circles. This view sees all biblical prophecy about the events leading up to Christ's second coming as fulfilled in the first century. At times it even argues that the second coming itself was fulfilled in Jesus' invisible coming in judgment on Israel in AD 70."

They attach to this statement a footnote that reads: "See esp. Kenneth L. Gentry, *He Shall Have Dominion*."[9]

---

[8] Ice in *PEBP*, 289. Emph. mine.

[9] Craig L. Blomberg and Sung Wook Chung, eds. *A Case for Historic Premillennialism: An Alternative to "Left Behind" Eschatology* (Grand Rapids: Baker, 2009), xv.

Now I will provide a brief, running critique of the problems within Hyper-preterism. These should be recognized by orthodox, Bible-believing Christians.

Creedal Failure

First, Hyper-preterism is definitionally heterodox in that it lies outside of creedal orthodoxy. No ecumenical creed of the church allows for the second advent occurring in AD 70.[10] "All of the major branches of Christendom firmly hold to the return of Jesus Christ to the abode of humanity."[11] Nor does any creed allow for dismissing the future bodily resurrection of believers. Nor do the creeds reduce the universal, personal judgment of all men at the end of history to a confined, representative judgment at the beginning of Christian history in AD 70.

In fact, "with the exception of the certainty of death, the one eschatological doctrine on which orthodox theologians most agree is the second coming of Christ."[12] It would be most remarkable if the entire church that came through AD 70 missed the proper understanding of the eschaton and did not realize its members had been resurrected. And that the next generation had no inkling of the great transformation that took place. Has the *entire* Christian church missed the *basic contours* of Christian eschatology for its first 1900 years? Has the "blessed hope" really been a "blasted hoax" all these years?

Second, Hyper-preterism has serious implications for the clarity of Scripture. This viewpoint not only has negative implications for the later creeds, but for the instructional abilities of the Apostles. Despite the Spirit-filled Apostles writing under divine inspiration, until very recently no one in church history understood the *major issues* of which they speak. Are the Scriptures *that* impenetrable on an issue of *that* significance (remember Hyper-preterism has built an entire, self-contained theology)?

On the Hyper-preterist view, Clement of Rome lives through AD 70 and yet has no idea he is resurrected, for he continues to look for a physical resurrection (*1 Clement* 50:3). Jude's (supposed) grandsons still seek a physical resurrection (cf. Eusebius, *Eccl. Hist.* 3:20:1ff). Whoever these

---

[10] For a more detailed examination of this matter, see ch 6 below.

[11] Gerhard Sauter, *Eschatological Rationality: Theological Issues in Focus* (Grand Rapids: Baker, 1996), 33.

[12] Millard J. Erickson, *Christian Theology* (2d. ed.: Grand Rapids: Baker/ Academic, 1998), 1192.

men are, they come right out of the first generation and from the land of Israel with absolutely no inkling of an AD 70 resurrection or a past second advent. See also the *Didache* 10:5; 16:1ff (first century); Ignatius, *Trallians* 9:2; *Smyrnaens* 2:1; 6:1; *Letter to Polycarp* 7:2 (early second century); Polycarp 2:1; 6:2; 7:1. See also Papias, Irenaeus, Justin Martyr.

Berkouwer rightly notes that the reason the resurrection finds early creedal acceptance is because of the New Testament's clear emphasis on it. The Hyper-preterist view has serious and embarrassing implications for the perspicuity of Scripture and the integrity of Christianity. And this despite the fact we are now (supposedly) in our resurrected states and have the outpoured Holy Spirit (Eph 4:8) and his gift of teachers (Eph 4:11), whom he gives to protect us from every wind of doctrine (Eph 4:12–14).

Third, the Hyper-preterist system leaves the new covenant Christian (in our post AD 70 era) without a canon. If AD 70 fulfills all prophecy and if the entire New Testament speaks to issues in the pre-AD 70 time frame, we do not have any directly relevant passages for us. The entire New Testament must be transposed before we can use it. Of course, we see a similar situation with the Old Testament. The Old Testament is directly designed for the old covenant people operating under the levitical system. But in the New Testament we have an interpretive word from God explaining the change in redemptive-history and interpreting the old covenant for us.

Hermeneutic Failure

Fourth, Hyper-preterism suffers from serious errors in its hermeneutical methodology. When a contextually defined passage applies to the AD 70 event, the Hyper-preterist will take *all* passages with *similar* language and apply them to AD 70, as well. But similarity does not imply identity. After all, Christ cleanses the temple twice and in virtually identical ways, but the two events are not the same — for one begins his ministry (John 2:13–17) while the other ends it (Matt 21:12–13).

Furthermore, we must distinguish *sense* and *referent*. For instance, several types of "resurrection" appear in Scripture: the dry bones of Ezekiel 37; spiritual redemption in John 5:24; physical redemption at the grave in John 5:28; Israel's renewal in Christ in Romans 11:15; and the beast's resurrection in Revelation 13:3. Orthodox preterists, however, hold that passages specifically delimiting the time-frame by temporal indicators (such as "this generation," "shortly," "at hand," "near," and similar wording) must apply to AD 70, but similar sounding passages may or may *not*.

Resurrection Errors

Fifth, their most serious error involves their removing the physical resurrection from systematic theology and the Christian hope. Paul specifically declares Christ's resurrection to be the paradigm of our own (1 Cor 15:20ff).[13] Yet we know that his was a physical, tangible resurrection (Luke 24:39), whereas ours is (in the Hyper-preterist's view) spiritual. What happens to the biblically-defined analogy between Christ's resurrection and ours in the Hyper-preterist system?

Sixth, numerous other theological and exegetical problems afflict a spiritual-only resurrection. For one thing, the Hyper-preterist view diminishes the significance of the bodily implications of sin: Adam's sin has *physical* effects, as well as judicial and spiritual effects. Where are these taken care of in the Hyper-preterist system? Death's implications are not just judicial and spiritual, but also physical (Gen 3:19; Matt 10:28; Rom 6:23). If Christians are *now* fulfilling the full resurrection expectation of Scripture, then the gnostics of the early Christian centuries were correct.

The physical world is superfluous in the Hyper-preterist viewpoint. The anthropology of Hyper-preterism is defective in this, not accounting for the theological significance of man's body/soul nature (Gen 2:7). This can also have implications for the person of Christ and the reality of his humanity.

Seventh, regarding the teaching of Christ and the Apostles, we must wonder why the Greeks mock Paul in Acts 17 for believing in the resurrection, if it were not a physical reality. We must wonder why Paul aligns himself with the Pharisees on the issue of the resurrection (Acts 23:6–9; 24:15, 21). We must wonder why we Christians still marry, since Christ teaches that in the resurrection we will *not* marry (Luke 20:35). We must wonder why the Apostles never correct the widespread notion of a physical resurrection so current in Judaism (cf. Josephus, Mishnah, Talmud, etc.).

Still further, we must wonder why we "resurrected" Christians must yet die. Why do we not leave this world like Enoch and Elijah? Furthermore, where and what is the resurrection of the lost (John 5:29; Acts

---

[13] See later exposition of this passage.

24:15)? Paul considers Hymeneaus and Philetus to be wrecking men's faith by saying the resurrection is past (2 Tim 2:17–18). A wrong view of the resurrection is a serious matter to Paul.

Eighth, practically we must wonder regarding the Hyper-preterist view: what difference our resurrection makes in this life? We get ill and are weak on the same scale as those prior to the AD 70 resurrection. Does this glorious resurrection of the "spiritual body" have no impact on our present condition? A Hyper-preterist analysis might leave us to expect that Paul looks to AD 70 as an agent of relief from the groanings and the temptations of the flesh (Rom 7:24; 8:19–24), yet we still have such — despite the only resurrection that system offers.

Christology Implications

Ninth, as noted previously, Acts 1 clearly defines Christ's second advent in terms of his ascension, which is a physical and visible event. For example, in Acts 1:8–11 Luke is careful to say the disciples are "beholding" him as he ascends; the cloud receives him "from the eyes of them" (v. 9b); they are "gazing" as he was "going" (v. 10); they are "looking" (v. 11); they "beheld" (v. 11). We know his ascension is a visible and glorious phenomenon involving his tangible resurrected body. And an actual visible cloud is associated with his ascension (v. 10).

Then we read that the angelic messengers resolutely declare "this same Jesus" (i.e., the Jesus they knew for over three years, who is now in a tangible resurrected body) will "so come *in like manner* as you saw Him go into heaven" (v. 11). The Greek *on tropon* literally means "what manner." The Greek phrase "never indicates mere certainty or vague resemblance; but wherever it occurs in the New Testament, denotes identity of mode or manner."[14] Thus, the angels do not simply say, "He will come again." But give a rather emphatic explanation, declaring that he "will come in just the same way as you have watched Him go into heaven." That is, just surely as your eyes saw this going, likewise his coming will be in that same visible manner.

As Peterson notes regarding Acts 1:9: These words "closely link the mission agenda of Jesus with his ascension and the angelic words that follow. 'Luke's point is that the missionary activity of the early church rested not only on Jesus' mandate but also on his living presence in heaven and

---

[14] J. A. Alexander, *The Acts of the Apostles Explained* (3rd ed. Grand Rapids: Zondervan, 1956 [rep. 1875]), *ad loc.*

the sure promise of his return.'"[15] Consequently, we have express biblical warrant to expect a visible, bodily, glorious return of Christ paralleling in kind the ascension. The Hyper-preterist position contradicts this clear teaching of Scripture.

Tenth, if AD 70 ends the Messianic reign of Christ (cf. Hyper-preterist view of 1Cor 15:24, 28), then the glorious Messianic era prophesied throughout the Old Testament is reduced to a forty year inter-regnum. Whereas by all biblical accounts, it is a lengthy, glorious era. The prophetical expressions of the kingdom tend to speak of an enormous period of time, even employing terms frequently used of eternity (2 Sam 7:13; Dan 2:44; Luke 1:33; Rev 11:15). Does Christ's kingdom parallel David's *exactly*, so that it only lasts for the same amount of time?

History and Church Errors

Eleventh, Hyper-preterists eternalize time — by allowing history to continue forever. This not only goes against express statements of Scripture, but also has God enduring a universe in which sin will dwell forever and ever and ever and ever and ever and ever and ever. God will never finally conclude man's rebellion; he will never finally reckon with sin.

Christ tells us that the judgment will be against rebels in their *bodies*, not spiritual bodies (Matt 10:28). The Hyper-preterist system does not reach back far enough (to the Fall and the curse on the physical world) to highlight the significance of redemption as it moves to a final, conclusive consummation, ridding the cursed world of sin. The full failure of the First Adam must be overcome by the full and final success of the Second Adam.

In addition, we have a problem regarding divine election. If history continues forever, the number of the elect is not a set figure. The elect becomes an ever growing number that never ceases. The Lamb's Book of Life becomes an unending recording rather than a set record.

Twelfth, Hyper-preterism has serious negative implications for ecclesiastical labor and worship. Shall we limit the Great Commission to the pre-AD 70 era, due to the interpretation of "the end" by Hyper-preterists? After all, Jesus commands: "teach them to observe all that I commanded you; and lo, I am with you always, even to the end of the age" (Matt 28:20).

---

[15] David G. Peterson, *The Acts of the Apostles* (Grand Rapids: Eerdmans, 2009), 114.

And is the Lord's Supper superfluous today, having been fulfilled in Christ's (alleged) second advent in AD 70? After all, Paul encourages us: "as often as you eat this bread and drink the cup, you proclaim the Lord's death until He comes" (1 Cor 11:26)?

These are just a few samples of the wide-ranging theological and historical problems facing Hyper-preterism. But now let us reflect on some particular Scriptures that are important to the dispute with the Hyper-preterists.

Conclusion

Clearly, a careful reading of the Hyper-preterist literature exposes its heterodox tendencies and convictions. And just as clearly, such a reading recognizes a strong distinction between (orthodox) preterism and Hyper-preterism. Christians cannot combat error if they themselves are confused and in error.

Chapter 3
THE FOUNDATIONAL TEXTS ANALYZED

In this chapter I will focus on a few of the Hyper-preterist's key passages. Their explanation of these biblical texts has been useful for drawing followers into the movement. And a proper understanding of these texts will be necessary for preventing others from stumbling into their system.

Luke 17:22–37

Matthew 24 is a key passage in the preterist understanding of Scripture. Hyper-preterists see this passage in its entirety as focusing on AD 70. Yet most (not all) orthodox preterists see Jesus as shifting their attention from AD 70 to the second advent in the transition passage at Matthew 24:34–36 (see ch 5 below for a detailed evidence for the transitional character and function of this passage).

One of the Hyper-preterist's leading arguments in making this observation is to point out that Luke 17 seems to mix up the material that we claim is so well-structured and sorted out in the two main sections of Matthew 24. And if this is so, then we no longer have any warrant for separating the two events.

As I begin considering this issue, it will be helpful to cite Luke 17:22–37 first:

> "And He said to the disciples, 'The days will come when you will long to see one of the days of the Son of Man, and you will not see it. They will say to you, "Look there! Look here!" Do not go away, and do not run after them. For just like the lightning, when it flashes out of one part of the sky, shines to the other part of the sky, so will the Son of Man be in His day. But first He must suffer many things and be rejected by this generation. And just as it happened in the days of Noah, so it will be also in the days of the Son of Man: they were eating, they were drinking, they were marrying, they were being given in marriage, until the day that Noah entered the ark, and the flood came and destroyed them all. It was the same as happened in the days of Lot: they were eating, they were drinking, they were buying, they were selling, they were planting, they were building; but on the day that Lot went out from Sodom it rained fire and brimstone from heaven and destroyed them all. It will be just the same on the day that the Son of Man is

> revealed. On that day, the one who is on the housetop and whose goods are in the house must not go down to take them out; and likewise the one who is in the field must not turn back. Remember Lot's wife. Whoever seeks to keep his life will lose it, and whoever loses his life will preserve it. I tell you, on that night there will be two in one bed; one will be taken and the other will be left. There will be two women grinding at the same place; one will be taken and the other will be left. [Two men will be in the field; one will be taken and the other will be left.] And answering they said to Him, 'Where, Lord?' And He said to them, 'Where the body is, there also the vultures will be gathered.'"

A quick reading of the fuller passage in Matthew 24:4–51 alongside of Luke 17:22–37 seems to demand that we drop any division in Matthew 24 at vv. 34–36. This suggests to the Hyper-preterist that there is, in fact, no distinction between AD 70 and the second advent. However, looks are deceiving. And this "problem" is not helpful to the Hyper-preterist argument. Note the following reply to Hyper-preterists on this point. I will organize the responses around specific questions.

Is a distinction crucial?

I must note up front that this issue is not really a crucial matter. Orthodox preterists see no doctrinal problems arising if we apply all of Matthew 24 to AD 70. We generally do not do so because of certain exegetical markers in the text, however. Yet if these are not sufficient to distinguish the latter part of Matthew 24 from the earlier part, it would not matter either to orthodox theology or to the preterist system. After all, (1) we find the second advent in numerous other passages (thus we are not ridding theology of the second coming of Christ), and (2) the AD 70 event is modeled on the second advent and is a distant adumbration of and pointer to it (so they are theologically linked and spoken of in similar fashion).

As I noted previously and will fully argue in the next chapter, however, I do believe we should recognize a transition from AD 70 to the distant second advent in Matthew 24:34–36. That being so, how do we explain the problem of Luke's "mixing up" the Matthew 24 material? This leads to my second question:

Are the passages the same?

Actually, the two texts record different sermons. The Lord presents the discourse recorded in Matthew 24 on the Mount of Olives (Matt 24:3) after looking out over Jerusalem (Matt 23:37). Whereas in Luke 17 he is on his way to Jerusalem (cf. Luke 17:11; 18:31; 19:11). In Matthew, Jesus is answering his *disciples* regarding their question about the temple's future (Matt 24:1–3). In Luke 17 he is interacting with the Pharisees (Luke 17:20–23) about the coming of the kingdom when he turns to speak to the disciples. No one is commenting on the temple, as in Matthew 24:1–2. In fact, we find Luke's version of the Olivet Discourse four chapters later in Luke 21:5–24.

As Morris notes regarding liberals who argue that Luke places this teaching in the wrong context: "It is much better to hold that ... Jesus [either] uttered the words on more than one occasion or ... Luke is correctly applying them to another situation."[1] So no matter what Jesus is speaking about, Luke is not shifting the material around. He is recording a different sermon altogether.

But there is more. We need also to ask:

Does similarity entail identity?

Similarity does not entail identity. That is, because *similar* prophecies occur in Matthew 24 as in Luke 17 does not mean they apply to the *same* events. Let me explain.

We see that similar expressions do not require identical realities. For instance, Scripture refers to Christ as a "lion" in some places (Rev 5:5), while in others it calls Satan a "lion" (1 Pet 5:8). Thus, the term "lion" can have different referents in different contexts, sometimes Christ, sometimes Satan.

Consider the prophetic concept of "the day of the Lord." In the Old Testament "the day of the Lord" occurs in several places and applies to different historical judgments. For instance, the day of the Lord comes upon Babylon, Idumea, and Judah (Isa 13:6, 9; Eze 13:5; Joel 1:15; 2:1, 11; Am 5:18, 20; Ob 15; Zep 1:7; Mal 4:5). Even though the language is the same (and why not, since all wars are basically similar?) and the phrase occurs in the singular (which suggests there is only one day of the Lord), these must be different events.

Is prophetic language stereotypical?

In Luke 17 Jesus is employing *stereotypical* language. By that I mean that some images are stereotypes that can apply to different events. For

---

[1] Leon Morris, *Acts* (*TNTC*) (Grand Rapids: Eerdmans, 1988), 286.

instance, though Sodom was an historical city that suffered God's historical judgment, the image of "Sodom" is used elsewhere in Scripture to picture man's cultural rebellion which deserves God's judgment. Therefore it can be used of evil cities even when not referring expressly to historical Sodom itself (Deut 29:23; Isa 1:9–10; 3:9; 13:19; Jer 23:14; 49:18; 50:40; Lam 4:6; Amos 4:11).

In this regard we should note Jesus' own reference to Lot from the Sodom episode (Luke 17:28–29, 32) and to Noah's flood (Luke 17:27; Matt 24:37–38). Like Sodom, the flood in Noah's day becomes an image of God's judgment in other contexts (Isa 54:9; Eze 14:14, 20; Heb 11:7; 1 Pet 3:20; 2 Pet 2:5).

Old Testament judgment language is often stereotyped so that it can apply to different historical episodes. For instance, in the historically distinct judgments upon Babylon, Edom, and Egypt, we read of the stars and moon being darkened or wasting away (Isa 13:1, 10; 34:4–5; Eze 32:2, 7–8). Using the Hyper-preterist approach we should argue that these are the same events because of the same language. But instead, scholars recognize the common use of stereotypes in prophecy.

Is Jesus using prophetic cameos?

Several of the images Jesus employs in Luke 17 and Matthew 24 are merely pointing out common life issues. In both chapters that we are considering, Jesus uses mundane activities as cameos of every day life. These are not alluding to historically datable events.

Consider, for instance, Christ's references to the two men in the field (Luke 17:36; Matt 24:40) or the two women grinding at a mill (Luke 17:35; Matt 24:41). These are portraits of daily life activities that will be caught up in and overwhelmed by God's judgment. Thus, these serve as compelling images of the disruption of daily life cycles, as in Exodus 11:5; Job 31:10; Isaiah 47:1–2. Undoubtedly, such will occur at the end of history just as it did in AD 70 — and just as it does in any war scenario.

Does Jesus repeat himself?

The record of the temple cleansing exposes the interpretive error involved in the Hyper-preterist argument. The Hyper-preterist is mistaken in arguing that inter-linking language is evidence that the same events are in view.

If you use this method you will conclude that the Gospels are in error in assigning a temple cleansing to the beginning of Christ's ministry (John

2:13–17) as well as to its end (Matt 21:12–13). The language is so similar that liberals say that one of the Gospels must be making a mistake by putting it in the wrong historical context. Yet the integrity of the Gospel record demands that Christ did this twice.

As a conference speaker I often use my materials over and over again. Because not everyone in the world has heard them. Jesus obviously did not have access to television and the Internet to hit everyone with his teaching simultaneously. He preached continuously over his three-year ministry, and not every word was recorded (John 21:25). So he uses his material repeatedly and adapts it to different situations. Luke 17 and Matthew 24 represent two different situations.

Conclusion to Luke 17 Analysis

Consequently, exegetical integrity does not require that similarities between Luke 17 and Matthew 24 anticipate the same events. More careful reflection on the two passages shows that the similar language can be applied to historically distinct episodes.

But now let us consider *the* foundational passage for the Hyper-preterist argument (which is also found in Luke's Gospel). Let us focus on:

Luke 21:22

Luke 21:22 is undoubtedly *the* key verse that Hyper-preterists use in promoting their unique understanding of the Bible, theology, and Christianity. In its context it reads as follows (the key phrase is *italicized*):

> When you see Jerusalem surrounded by armies, then recognize that her desolation is at hand. Then let those who are in Judea flee to the mountains, and let those who are in the midst of the city depart, and let not those who are in the country enter the city; because these are days of vengeance, in order that *all things which are written may be fulfilled*. (Luke 21:20–22)

Inarguably, the context here is focusing on AD 70, as even dispensationalists agree. And we certainly can see why the Hyper-preterists attempt to use this text as a basis for their new theology.

They wrongly interpret the statement as if Jesus is speaking *universally* of absolutely *all* prophecies that have *ever* been written when he states that "all things which are written" will be fulfilled in AD 70. They hold, therefore, that *no* prophecy remains. This would mean that prophecies regarding the resurrection of all men, the second coming, and more came to pass in AD 70. Unfortunately, they base their argument on deficient hermeneutics. Consider the following observations.

The particular context

The context explains the particular "all things" Christ has in mind. He is *not* speaking universally of absolutely all biblical prophecy. He is referring only to the judgment prophecies *regarding Jerusalem's destruction*.

Note that the disciples' pointing out the temple's stones sparks the discourse (Luke 21:5). Then Jesus declares that "these things" will not be left one upon another (21:6). Then the disciples ask "when therefore will *these things* be?" (21:7). Jesus responds with the prophecy regarding *Jerusalem's* destruction (21:8–24), for he is dealing with Jerusalem's surrounding and desolation (21:20). Then he declares "*these* are the days of vengeance, in order that all things which are written may be fulfilled" (21:22). Clearly his focus is on Jerusalem and her temple.

The specific wording

The word "all" in Luke 21:22 does not necessarily entail an all-inclusive universal. For instance, in Matthew 3:5 we read of the response to John the Baptist: "then Jerusalem was going out to him, and *all* Judea, and *all* the district around the Jordan." No one argues that each and every man, woman, and infant including those who were lame, dying, or mentally incompetent came out to John.

Also consider Matthew 13:32. There Jesus declares that the mustard seed "is smaller than *all* other seeds," even though it manifestly is not. The orchid seed is almost as small as dust (1/200 of an inch), and therefore much smaller than the mustard seed (1/20 of an inch). Is Jesus mistaken? No. Undoubtedly, Jesus is referring to a limited "all," i.e., all seeds that a local farmer might regularly sow in his garden. He is speaking proverbially rather than absolutely; he is preaching a sermon not providing a botanical lecture.[2] Jesus does the same in Matthew 17:20 where he promises that faith as small as a mustard seed can move a mountain.

---

[2] Some evangelical scholars (wrongly) deem this to be an example of Jesus simply accommodating the mistaken views of antiquity and passing them on to his hearers as if factual, though erroneous. Denis O. Lamoureux in Matthew Barrett and Ardel B. Caneday, eds., *Four Views on the Historical Adam* (Grand Rapids: Zondervan, 2013), 60.

In fact, we also know that — despite his statement in Matthew 13:32— the mustard plant was not the largest garden plant, for the olive tree could grow almost twice as tall. And Jesus surely knew that.

On and on we could go with illustrations. Clearly the word "all" does not necessarily mean "each-and-every" one. And as I note in the preceding point, Luke 17:22 surely refers only to prophecies regarding Jerusalem's destruction.

The particular absurdity

On the Hyper-preterist exegesis Christ's statement would be erroneous to the point of absurdity. Are "all" prophecies fulfilled in AD 70?

What about the virgin birth (Isa 7:14; Matt 1:22–23)? Christ's crucifixion (Luke 24:26–27)? His resurrection (Luke 24:45–47)? After all, also appearing in Luke's Gospel is the Lord's statement regarding his crucifixion — which occurred long before AD 70: "For I tell you that this which is written must be fulfilled in Me, 'and he was numbered with transgressors'; for that which refers to Me has its fulfillment" (Luke 22:37). These prophecies are certainly "written" in the Old Testament. Yet they clearly are fulfilled *before* AD 70.

The particular grammar

The specific grammar of the passage limits the declaration. How is this so?

Note that Jesus speaks of "all things which are written." He does this by employing a perfect passive participle: *gegrammena* ("having been written"). This refers to prophecies *already* written — *when he speaks in AD 30.* Yet we know that more prophecies arise later in the New Testament revelation.

Once again we see a limitation on Jesus' statement. Furthermore, technically it does not even refer to any prophecy which Christ *speaks*. For these are not prophecies that have already been *written* when he speaks around AD 30. The books of the New Testament were written several years after he ministered, well after he spoke.

Thus, Jesus is referring to all things written *in the Old Testament*. At this stage of redemptive history those are the only prophecies that had already been written.

Conclusion to Luke 21 analysis

So then, the key verse supporting Hyper-preterism does not function like they think. Though Hyper-preterism has an apparent textual foundation, looks are deceiving. A closer examination of their key proof-text shows they have built their house on the sand. Thus, when the flood and the winds of critical analysis slam against their house, great is its fall.

Conclusion

These two texts in Luke's Gospel both derive from the Lord Jesus himself.

Luke 17 can truly confuse the incautious reader of the Gospel. Nevertheless, an improper reading does not necessarily distort biblical theology and lead to a false theological construct. There is a legitimate debate over whether Matthew 24:34–36 represents a transition from near-term events to long-distance ones. And that debate necessarily impacts our understanding of Luke 17. However, I believe a strong case can be made for maintaining a division in Matthew 24 despite the difficulty Luke 17 seems to present.

Yet for 2000 years Luke 21:22 was well understood in orthodox Christianity. It never posed any threat to basic Bible doctrine. It has only recently been wrenched from its context to develop a bold, new theology. We need to keep it in context in order to keep ourselves in orthodox Christianity.

Chapter 4
THE RESURRECTION TEXTS CONSIDERED

As we continue our analysis of the Hyper-preterist theological system, we must recognize the enormous significance of Christ's resurrection for a truly biblical theology and an accurate Christian worldview. To illustrate this I will deal with just one of the redemptive-historical *effects* of his resurrection: the eschatological resurrection of believers. Christ's resurrection not only secures our present redemption *for* glory (Rom 4:25; 10:9–10) but our future resurrection *to* glory (Rom 8:23).

As I noted previously one major feature of Hyper-preterism is its denying the believer's future physical resurrection at the end of history. As I will show, this contradicts a major result of the resurrection of Christ. Before I demonstrate this I must briefly summarize the argument for Christ's *physical* resurrection, which is the effective cause of our own future resurrection.

The Scriptures teach that Christ arises from the dead in the same body in which he dies (John 2:18–19, 21). As such, it miraculously attests to the truth of his divine mission on earth (Matt 12:39–40). This is why his disciples find the tomb and his burial clothing empty, for when he arises, his physical body departs from them (Matt 28:6; John 20:4–11, 15). The gospels present the resurrected Christ in a material body that men can touch and handle (Luke 24:39), which still has the wounds of the cross (John 20:27), to which people can cling (John 20:17; Matt 28:9), and which can eat food (Luke 24:42–43; John 21:11–14).

Christianity affirms Christ's corporeal resurrection as a prominent feature of its high supernaturalism and eschatological orientation. But how does that speak to the issue of *our* resurrection? I will simply provide an abbreviated commentary on two important resurrection texts, Daniel 12 and 1 Corinthians 15. Both of these speak directly to the point and are favorite passages for Hyper-preterists.

Daniel 12:1–2

Daniel 12 presents us with another prophecy that is seized upon by Hyper-preterists. They see Daniel 12:1–2 as confirming their view that the eschatological resurrection occurs in the first-century in the historical context of the destruction of the temple.

Daniel 12:1 seems clearly enough to be speaking of the great tribulation that occurs in AD 70 (cp. Matt 24:21; cf. vv. 2, 34):

> Now at that time Michael, the great prince who stands guard over the sons of your people, will arise. And there will be a time of distress such as never occurred since there was a nation until that time; and at that time your people, everyone who is found written in the book, will be rescued.

How shall we understand this text? In order to set up the matter before us, let us begin by noting:

The "problem" in Daniel 12:1–2

Daniel does seem to be speaking of the AD 70 tribulation. But he also appears to speak of the eschatological resurrection, as if it occurs at that time: "And many of those who sleep in the dust of the ground will awake, these to everlasting life, but the others to disgrace and everlasting contempt" (Dan 12:2).

How are we to understand this short passage? Does Daniel teach that the eschatological, consummate resurrection occurs during the great tribulation in AD 70? Does his prophecy serve as evidence that the resurrection is not a literal, consummate resurrection — since a resurrection of those whose names are "written in the book" does not occur then, and since whatever resurrection he speaks of occurs in the first century instead of the last?

This passages does not offer support to the Hyper-preterist thesis. Let me explain.

The explanation of Daniel 12:1–2

Daniel appears to be presenting Israel as a grave site under God's curse: Israel as a corporate body is in the "dust" (Dan 12:2). Dust is often associated with death and the grave (Gen 3:19; Job 7:21; 17:16; 20:11; 21:26; Isa 29:4; 26:19). In this he follows Ezekiel's pattern in his vision of the dry bones, which represent Israel's "death" in the Babylonian dispersion (Eze 37).[1] If this is so, then Daniel 12 would not *directly* teach individual, bodily resurrection at that time. (Nevertheless, the fact that it uses such language shows that a literal bodily resurrection lies behind the image, and so it *indirectly* affirms the future bodily resurrection.)

---

[1] See: *DBPET*, 148.

In Daniel's prophecy many will awaken, as it were, to enjoy God's grace in receiving everlasting life. Having trusted in Christ, they will escape God's judgment by fleeing from Jerusalem (see explanation below). While at the same time others will suffer the fury of God's wrath as he destroys them historically and sends them into eternity to suffer "everlasting contempt."

In the New Testament Simeon employs similar imagery of division that results from one's response to Christ in Luke 2:34. There he prophesies the results of Jesus's birth for Israel: "And Simeon blessed them, and said to Mary His mother, 'Behold, this Child is appointed for the fall and rise of many in Israel, and for a sign to be opposed.'" Many will be blessed by Christ ("rise of many") and many will be judged ("the fall ... of many"). This prophecy of the sorting out of the Jews in Israel comes to historical fulfillment in the destruction of the temple and Jerusalem in AD 70.

Christ himself points out that some from Israel will believe and be saved, while others will not (e.g., Matt 10:34–36; 13:11–15). He also teaches that in the removing of the kingdom from Israel because of their rejecting him, many will be crushed and scattered like dust (Matt 21:43–45). He even speaks of the saved Jews as arising from the "shadow of death" (Matt 4:16).

Though in AD 70 elect Jews will flee Israel and will live (Matt 24:16, 22), the rest of the nation will become a corpse: "wherever the corpse is, there the vultures will gather" (Matt 24:28; cp. Luke 17:37). Indeed, in AD 70 we see in the destruction of the city of Jerusalem (Matt 22:7) that "many are called, but few are chosen" (Matt 22:14).[2]

Elsewhere the Lord employs the image of "regeneration" to the arising of the new Israel from out of dead, old covenant Israel in AD 70: "You who have followed Me, in the regeneration when the Son of Man will sit on his glorious throne, you also shall sit upon twelve thrones, judging the twelve tribes of Israel" (Matt 19:28). That is, as the new covenant is forever established in the passing away of the old covenant temple system in AD 70 (Heb 8:13), the apostles will oversee Israel's judgment.

This paralleling of divine blessing and divine curse, of life and death (cf. Rom 11:15) for those in Israel is a frequent theme (under varied images) in the Book of Revelation: God's angels protect some Jews from

---

[2] See Matt 22:1–13 as an image of God's inviting Jews to Christ, which invitation Israel rejects.

the winds of judgment (those who are sealed), while not protecting others (Rev 7:1–9). John measures some Jews for safe-keeping in the temple, while not measuring others (11:1–2). Some stand high upon Mount Zion in safety (14:1–5), while others do not (14:17–20).

Returning to Daniel, it appears that Daniel is drawing from the hope of the future, literal resurrection and applying it symbolically to the first century leading up to the tribulation in AD 70. That is, he pictures God's winnowing of Israel in AD 70 (Matt 3:12).

Again, this is much like Ezekiel's practice in his vision of the valley of dry bones. Though Ezekiel's prophecy is concerned with Israel as a whole, Daniel shows that Israel's hope lies in the believing remnant.

In Daniel 12:4 the prophet hears a command to seal up his message until Israel's end, thus delaying its prophesied actions. In Revelation 22:10 John receives a command precisely the opposite of Daniel's, resulting in Revelation as a whole being opened and thereby fulfilled shortly: "Do not seal up the words of the prophecy of this book, for the time is near" (Rev 22:10; cp. 1:1, 3; 22:6). And as we saw earlier, Revelation is largely about the AD 70 destruction of the temple and Jerusalem.

Then Daniel sees in 12:5–7 an image that forms the pattern of John's vision in Revelation 10:5. A man (angel) standing above the waters uttering an oath to the eternal God. He promises that the events of Israel's end will be finished, transpiring within a period of "a time, times, and half a time." This apparently signifies a period of one year, two years, and half a year, which is John's three and one-half years or forty-two months (Rev 11:2; cp. Rev 12:14). That was the length of the Jewish War with Rome from its formal engagement in February AD 67 by Nero Caesar until the destruction of the temple in August AD 70.[3]

In this chapter Daniel expresses confusion about the outcome of his prophecy. He knows neither *when* (Dan 12:6) nor *how* (Dan 12:8) these prophecies will come to pass. But according to Revelation 10:6–7, John is informed both *when* and *how* they will transpire. This is because John lives in the end-time period (beginning with Christ's incarnation, Acts 2:16–17; 1 Cor 10:11; 2 Tim 3:1; Heb 1:1–2; 9:26; 1 Jn 2:18; 1 Pet 1:20).

---

[3] Bunson states that Vespasian "was given command of the legions in Palestine in February 67, the rank of governor of Judaea, and the task of suppressing the revolt of the Jews." Matthew Bunson, *A Dictionary of the Roman Empire* (Oxford: University Press, 1991), 443.

Conclusion

As we have seen, the resurrection in Daniel 12 does not support the Hyper-preterist approach. This is because it does not associate the *consummate* resurrection with the AD 70 tribulation. Rather Daniel only picks up on resurrection imagery and, like Ezekiel, applies that to corporate Israel. He is teaching that in the events of AD 70, the true Israel will arise from old Israel's carcass, as if in a resurrection.

Acts 24:15

In Acts 24:14–15 we come upon another passage that is significant to the debate between orthodoxy and heterodoxy regarding the resurrection. There Paul writes:

> But this I admit to you, that according to the Way which they call a sect I do serve the God of our fathers, believing everything that is in accordance with the Law and that is written in the Prophets; having a hope in God, which these men cherish themselves, that there shall certainly be a resurrection of both the righteous and the wicked.

This text is re-interpreted by Hyper-preterists in order to counter the historic Christian position on the resurrection. The supposed evidence that the Hyper-preterist draws from this text is found in the Greek phrase that is here translated: "there shall certainly be a resurrection." The Greek words behind this English translation are: *anastasin mellein esesthai*.

Hyper-preterism seizes upon the word *mellein* (from the Greek verb *mello*) and argues that it should be translated "about to." That is, they would translate this phrase: "there is about to be a resurrection." According to them, therefore, Paul is stating that he is expecting the resurrection to occur soon (i.e., at AD 70).

Unfortunately for the Hyper-preterist, this is a misreading of Paul that they wrongly employ to support their theological error. Let me explain.

Lexical data

First, lexically the word *mello* has several possible meanings. That is, it does not simply mean "about to," as the Hyper-preterist argument requires. Indeed, it is a rather ambiguous term. Greek scholar Daniel B. Wallace has written an important Greek grammar titled, *Greek Grammar: Beyond the Basics: An Exegetical Syntax of the New Testament* (1996). On p. 536 of this work he speaks of "the ambiguity of the lexical nuance of *mello* (which usually means either 'I am about to' [immediacy] or 'I will inevitably' [certainty])."

This is widely recognized by lexicographers. For instance, the *Exegetical Dictionary of the New Testament* (2:404) declares: "Clearly ... *mello* does not always have a fixed meaning."

Below I will cite a few technical sources for the definition and explanation of *mello*. Please be aware: when I cite these lexical sources I will expand the abbreviated (space-saving) terms rather than encumber the reader with [bracketed] expansions. Other than this, the citations are exact.

The Baur-Arndt-Gingrich-Danker *Lexicon* exposes some of the ambiguity by offering the following definitions of *mello*:

> "1. to take place a future point of time and so to be subsequent to another event, be about to, used with an infinitive following.... 2. to be inevitable, be destined, inevitable.... 3. The participle is used absolutely in the meaning (in the) future, to come.... 4. delay...."

In the Louw-Nida *Greek-English Lexicon of the New Testament Based on Semantic Domains* (vol. 1) we read the three leading meanings of *mello*:

> "*mello*: to occur at a point of time in the future which is subsequent to another event and closely related to it — 'to be about to.'" (p. 636)
>
> "*mello*: to be inevitable, with respect to future development — 'must be, has to be.'" (p. 672)
>
> "*mello*: to extend time unduly, with the implications of lack of decision — 'to wait, to delay.'" (p. 646).

In the *Exegetical Dictionary of the New Testament* (2:403) we read the following definitions: "intend, be about to, will (as auxiliary verb for the future), be destined to; consider, hesitate, delay."

The ambiguity of *mello* is clearly seen in these lexical definitions. The term can even have opposite meanings, speaking either of a soon-coming event or a delay! It is not helpful to a new movement to base an important argument on the single appearance of an ambiguous verb in an attempt to overthrow 2000 years of Christian orthodoxy. This lexical evidence alone renders void this particular Hyper-preterist argument. But this evidence does not stand alone: there is more!

Syntactical data

Second, syntactically when *mello* appears in conjunction with a future infinitive (as here in Acts 24:15) it indicates certainty. In Acts 24:15 *mello* appears as *mellein*, a present active infinite, which becomes a helping verb for the immediately following word *esesthai*, the future middle infinitive of *eimi* ("to be").

The Baur-Arndt-Gingrich-Danker *Lexicon* states: "With the future infinitive *mello* denotes certainty that an event will occur in the future."

The phrase appearing in Acts 24:15 occurs only two other times in the New Testament (Acts 11:28 and 27:10). But it also appears in Josephus, and in a closely related construction in Diognetus.

In Acts 27:10 Paul warns the captain of the ship he was on: "Men, I perceive that the voyage will certainly be [*mellein esesthai*] with damage and great loss." The pilot and the captain of the ship disagreed and forged ahead. Paul was prophesying the ship's wrecking as a certain event.

In Acts 11:28 Agabus prophesies "that there would certainly be [*mellein esesthai*] a great famine all over the world." And we read that it most certainly did come to pass in the reign of Claudius.

In fact, in the *Exegetical Dictionary of the New Testament* (2:403) we read that "in Acts mello contains no suggestion of a near future."

In Josephus's *Antiquities of the Jews* 13:12:1 the same phrase is used of a certain future occurrence:

> "The occasion of which hatred is thus reported: when Hyrcanus chiefly loved the two eldest of his sons, Antigonus and Aristobutus, God appeared to him in his sleep, of whom he inquired which of his sons should be his successor. Upon God's representing to him the countenance of Alexander, he was grieved that he was to be the heir of all his goods, and suffered him to be brought up in Galilee. However, God did not deceive Hyrcanus; for after the death of Aristobulus, he certainly [*mellei esesthai*] took the kingdom."

In Diognetus 8:2 we read: "Dost thou accept the empty and non-sensical statements of those pretentious philosophers: of whom some said that God was fire (they call that God, whereunto they themselves shall go [*mellousi choresein*], and others water, and others some other of the elements which were created by God?"

This is why none — not *one* — of the standard translations of the Acts 24:15 translate *mello* as expressing nearness. Rather they translate it simply as a future, certain event (see: KJV, ESV, NEB, NIV, NAB, NKJV, NRSV, etc.). The NASB (cited above) has an excellent rendering: "having a hope in God, which these men cherish themselves, that there shall certainly be a resurrection of both the righteous and the wicked."

This is why, also, we do not find Acts 24:15 used by liberals to show the error of prophecy in the Bible. That is, no liberal commentator points to this verse as evidence that Paul made a mistake, though they point out other near-term passages as involving error (though they wrongly interpret those texts): texts such as Mark 9:1 and Matthew 24:34.

For instance, we note that Mark 9:1 is brought up as an error for expecting the near-term return of Christ in: *The Intepreter's Bible*, *The New Century Bible Commentary*, and *Meyer's New Testament Commentary*. But Acts 24:15 is never mentioned as such in these commentaries.

Contextual data

Third, contextually: Paul's argument in Acts 24 supports this idiomatic usage of the certainty of the resurrection, rather than of its nearness.

Paul is on trial for his life, having been brought to court by Jews. His clever maneuver is to divide his opponents against themselves: the Pharisees believe in a resurrection of the dead; the Sadducees do not (cp. Acts 23:6–7). Thus, Paul argues for the certainty of the resurrection (by use of this idiomatic expression, *mello esesthai*) and concludes: "For the resurrection of the dead I am on trial before you today" (Acts 24:21). He is not on trial for declaring the resurrection is near, but is attempting to gain the hearing of the Pharisees over against the Sadducees on the fact of the resurrection.

Note also a little more fully what he states as he defends his Christianity (called "the Way"): "But this I admit to you, that according to the Way which they call a sect I do serve the God of our fathers, believing everything that is in accordance with the Law and that is written in the Prophets; having a hope in God, which these men cherish themselves, that there shall certainly be a resurrection of both the righteous and the wicked" (Acts 24:14–15).

Consider two further important observations: Here he is asserting the resurrection as (1) a fact of Scripture (i.e., the Old Testament) and (2) as being held by the Jews (the Pharisees and their followers) themselves. He declares it a fact of Scripture when he states: "believing everything that is in accordance with the Law and that is written in the Prophets." And he also declares that "these men cherish [this truth] themselves." We see the resurrection in the Old Testament (e.g., Job 19:25–27; Isa 26:19) and in intertestamental Judaism (e.g., 2 Macc 7:9, 14, 23; 12:43; 1 Enoch 51:1; Josephus, *Wars of the Jews* 2:8:14; *Antiquities* 18:1:3).

He is surely not arguing that the Old Testament prophesied that the resurrection would occur "soon"! Nor would he be affirming that the Pharisees believed it was fast approaching. He is speaking of its certainty not its nearness. Thus, the Hyper-preterist use of this verse is erroneous.

1 Corinthians 15

The Corinthian context and problem

Before surveying this chapter we must be aware of a major underlying problem in this church located in the Greek city of Corinth: a mixture of a quasi-gnostic philosophy (highlighting higher knowledge and denigrating the physical realm) and an exorbitant pride rooted in spiritual-eschatological claims.

Indeed, Paul opens his letter by referring to their spiritual gifts (1 Cor 1:7; cp. chs. 12–14) and the matter of a Greek concern for "knowledge" (1:18–25; cp. chs. 2–4, 8–10). These issues almost invariably lie behind the particular problems he addresses. For example, their sexual immorality is rooted in their unconcern with issues of physical morality (6:13, 15; "the body doesn't matter! what's the problem?") and their denial of legitimate sexual relations in marriage (7:1–4; "we are above physical relations"). And their charismatic abuses are quite well-known (chs 12–14).

The Corinthian gnostics even revolt against local social conventions and boundary markers in disregarding public decorum in dress (hair style) by their "eschatological women" (1 Cor 11; see Gordon Fee's commentary on 1 Corinthians). These women assert that since the eschaton (end-time) has come, then the resurrection is past — consequently, they are like the angels in heaven who have no need of marriage nor differentiation from males (based on Matt 22:30).

Introducing the problem and the solution

In 1 Corinthians 15 Paul focuses on a denial of the resurrection of the body. In the first part of his argument for the resurrection (1 Cor 15:1–34) he repeatedly expresses his concern for its *necessity*: "if the dead are not raised" (vv. 12, 13, 15, 16, 29, 32). To dispel all doubt about our resurrection he links Christ's resurrection to ours (as elsewhere: Rom 8:34–37; 1 Cor 6:14; Phil 3:21). As we will see, this linkage powerfully affirms the physical resurrection.

In the second part of his response (1 Cor 15:35–57) Paul adapts his argument for the resurrection to the pneumatic-eschatological theology of his audience. He rebuts them by responding to their spiritual pride regarding "knowledge" and "gifts." He argues that *they themselves* have not yet received the full pneumatic (i.e., spiritual) blessings of redemption (and neither will they in a few weeks, as per the ludicrous Hyper-preterist AD 70 scheme).

Indeed, these pneumatic-Christians will not attain the fullest expression of the Holy Spirit until "the end" (1 Cor 15:24a), at the consummation (v. 24b–28), following upon the resurrection of the dead (vv. 21–23). Effectively Paul not only corrects their present dismissal of the importance of the material order, but affirms their future eternal materiality in a physical body!

Paul's first argument

After insisting that Christ is resurrected from the dead and that this is the foundation of our redemptive hope (1 Cor 15:1–19), Paul then powerfully links our resurrection to Christ's. In other words, his whole point regarding Christ's resurrection is to lay a foundation for ours. In verse 20 we read: "But now Christ has been raised from the dead, the *first fruits* (Gk., *aparche*) of those who are asleep." This first fruits imagery carries a load of theological implications regarding our physical resurrection.

First, the temporal significance of "first" requires that Christ's resurrection is peculiarly the first of its kind. No other consummate-order resurrection occurs before his. Second, in that he is the "first fruit" he *represents* the rest, just as the Old Testament offering of the first part of the harvest represents the whole harvest (cp. Rom 11:16). Christ's resurrection represents our own. Third, the "first fruit" also promises more to come. Christ's is unique for the time, but it points to others to follow at "the end" (1 Cor 15:24). Thus, the resurrection of Christ as the first fruits is: (1) the first of this order to occur, (2) represents his people's resurrection, and (3) expects more eschatological resurrections to follow at the end.

Consequently, the *fact* of Christ's resurrection is essential to the believer's resurrection — *and anticipates it.* From Adam arises death and all of its processes; so from Christ arises life and its fullest blessings (1 Cor 15:21–28). Christ's resurrection is necessary for the triumph of life over death (vv. 25–26), which we will finally and fully enjoy only when we ourselves arise from the dead, wherein Christ defeats the "last enemy" (v. 26). This is fundamentally important to Paul.

In 1 Corinthians 15:29–34 Paul presents a relentless and vigorous *ad hominem* against his Corinthian opponents: He notes he is risking his life for what the Corinthians deny (1 Cor 15:30–32). He lashes out against their spiritual pride in thinking they have arrived at the fullness of Holy Spirit blessings (v. 33). He warns that their "bad company" on this matter has "corrupted good morals" (v. 33; cp. 1 Cor 6–7 particularly). They must become "sober" and "stop sinning" in this (v. 34). And all of this in the context of his argument for the resurrection of believers!

Thus, once we determine the nature of Christ's resurrection, we understand the nature of our own. If Christ physically arises from the dead, then so shall we, for he is the "first fruits" of our resurrection. The only way around our physical resurrection is to deny Christ's physical resurrection.

Paul's second argument

Paul finally arrives at the specific objection toward which he is driving: "But someone will say, 'How are the dead raised? And with what kind of body do they come?'" (1 Cor 15:35). Here he is clearly speaking of a physical resurrection in that: (1) His opening question concerns how the "dead" are "raised," that is, "with what kind of *body*"? (2) The verb "raised" is attached to "the dead" in verses 1–34, and to their actual "bodies" in verses 35–58. And since he is dealing with their objection regarding a physical resurrection, he now emphasizes the "body" (*soma*) in this portion of his argument (vv. 35, 37, 38, 40, 42, 44). (3) Christ's resurrection from "the dead" is the key to the whole passage and argument (vv. 12, 13, 15–16), and his was a physical resurrection. In fact, Paul mentions Christ's resurrection in the context of his being "dead," "buried," and "raised." Christ's *body* was buried; so his *body* is what raised.

Contrary to their quasi-gnostic, hyper-spiritual, eschatologically-focused claims, Paul establishes the death of the body as the pre-condition for the fullness of the life they presently claim. He illustrates this by the seed that is sown, which must "die" (1 Cor 15:36–37) so that it can arise to eschatological glory. Despite their pride of "having arrived," the pneumatic Christians cannot "be there" yet. Their bodies haven't been "sown."

In 1 Corinthians 15:38–41 Paul emphasizes two crucial truths in response to their question (v. 35): (1) "*God* gives it a body just as *he* wished" (v. 38a). As with Augustine later, all objectors must recognize: "Is he who was able to make you when you did not exist not able to make over what you once were?" (*Sermons on Ascension*, 264:6). Any objection regarding the difficulty of resurrecting a dead body is more than accounted for by the fact that it is God who effects it.

(2) God gives bodies appropriate to their environment (1 Cor 15:38b). He gives fish bodies appropriate to water, birds appropriate to flight, and

so on (vv. 39–41). And all bodies have a level of "glory" appropriate to their estate (vv. 40–41), whether they be "earthly" or "heavenly" (v. 40). Christ adapts the glorious condition of the resurrected body for victory over the decay element. Though our pre-eschatological condition suffers dishonor and weakness, our future estate will enjoy glory and power (vv. 43–44; cp. Rom 8:11; 2 Cor 4:7–12; Phil 3:21). In fact, it is "the body" itself that Christ will transform from being perishable to imperishable (vv. 42, 52–54).

Paul employs shock therapy against these pneumatics: "It is sown a natural body, it is raised a spiritual body. If there is a natural body, there is also a spiritual body" (1 Cor 15:44). His point appears to be that not only should they not denigrate the present material order (which they do, chs. 6–7), but he informs them that they will arise again in a "spiritual *body*" in the eschatological order! And here is where the Hyper-preterist theological naivete causes them to stumble so badly.

Hyper-preterists believe Paul's reference to the "spiritual body" speaks of the *substance* of the body, its compositional makeup. Consequently, they boldly employ this verse for discounting a physical resurrection. Of course, this is as wrong-headed as to say a Coca-Cola bottle is made of Coca-Cola. Note the following evidences supporting the orthodox approach to Paul's argument (to name but a few):

(1) This "spiritual [*pneumatikos*] body" is no more immaterial than the "natural [*psuchikos*] body," even though both "spirit" (*pneuma*) and "soul" (*psuche*) often refer to the immaterial element within. Here Paul uses these (usually spiritual) terms to describe the *body*, and we know that our present natural (*psuchikos*) body is material. In 1 Corinthians 2:14 these adjectives distinguish the believer and the unbeliever. Rather than distinguishing their *body materials*, the terms focus on their *driving forces*: spiritual (Spirit-driven) concerns over against animal appetites.

(2) In Paul the semantic domain for *pneuma* overwhelming means "pertaining to the Holy Spirit" (e.g., 1 Cor 2:13; 3:1; 12:1; Rom 1:11; Eph 1:3; 5:19). That is, *governed by* the Spirit of God. The adjectives *psuchikos* and *pneumatikos* describe, therefore, the essential *governing* characteristic of each body: the present, unresurrected, fallen *body* over against the future, resurrected, redeemed *body*. That is, they speak of the earth-related, animal-appetite-controlled *condition* of the present order (the totality of man in his earthly estate) over against the eternity-related, Holy Spirit-controlled condition of the resurrected estate (the totality of man in his eternal estate).

The glory of the eschatological state entered into by the eschatological resurrection involves the full dominance of the Holy Spirit and all that that entails (including the body's imperishable condition and its moral control). And contextually, Paul designs his response to confront the prideful Corinthian pneumatics who think they have arrived at full spiritual glory. (Later Paul will note that the natural is first, not the spiritual, showing that the Corinthians must first live out their present lives before attaining the fullness of the Spirit, 1 Cor 15:46).

(3) Paul's parallels and contrasts show his concern is not physical versus immaterial, but perishable versus imperishable (1 Cor 15:42), dishonor versus honor (v. 43a), and weakness versus power (v. 43b). Our resurrected condition will be so governed by the Holy Spirit that the weaknesses of our present condition will be totally overcome by the transformational power of the Spirit. Indeed, he emphasizes the difference of *glory* as the key (vv. 40–41).

Similarly, we should note that *psychikos* ("natural") and *pneumatikos* ("spiritual") is contrasted in 1 Corinthians 2:14–15 in such a way as to confirm this. There the natural man (the unbeliever) is not a person in a material body as over against the spiritual man (the believer) who is in a spiritual body. Rather, he is one who is controlled by the Holy Spirit. Thus, "the transformed body, therefore, is not composed of 'spirit'; it is a *body* adapted to the eschatological existence that is under the ultimate domination of the Spirit."[4]

(4) According to scholars such as A. T. Robertson, adjectives ending in *-inos* generally denote compositional material, whereas those ending with *-ikos* signify characteristics. This fits the flow of Paul's argument regarding the "natural"(*psuchikos*) and the "spiritual" (*pneumatikos*) body as I present it above — and it supports the historic faith of the church regarding the resurrection.

(5) Once again Paul brings in the parallel between Adam and Christ as illustrating the differing circumstances of our estates (1 Cor 15:45–48). In v. 45 he applies Genesis 2:7 in light of his resurrection argument, contrasting the Adamic condition (the first Adam) with the resurrected Christ (the second Adam). (He cites the Septuagint: "the man became a living [*psuchen*] soul.") Adam's body was a *psuchen* body subject to animal weaknesses (hunger, death, and so forth, Gen 1:29; 2:17). Thus, we have

---

[4] Gordon D. Fee, *The First Epistle to the Corinthians* (NICNT) (Grand Rapids: Eerdmans, 1987), 786.

the distinction between the *psuche* (soul) and *pneuma* (spirit): But we know that Adam was not immaterial, nor was Christ in his resurrection. The idea here is that just as Adam is the source of our perishable bodies as the "first Adam," so Christ is the source of our Spirit-powered bodies as the "last Adam" (the man of the last estate or condition of the redeemed). Thus, Paul is drawing the parallel between the two material bodies and their consequent conditions (cp. v. 22), then noting the superiority of the consummate state represented in Christ's resurrection condition.

(6) In 1 Corinthians 15:47 ("the first man is from the earth, earthy; the second man is from heaven") Paul is not speaking of the origin of Adam and of Christ, but the *quality* of their conditions (focusing on the *resurrected* Christ). He is reiterating the difference between their weakness/power, inglorious/glorious conditions. Resurrected believers share the heavenly life of Christ but are not *from* heaven themselves. Paul contrasts the resurrection body with the Genesis 2:7 Adam (vv. 45–46). Thus, "just as we have borne the image of the earthy, we shall also bear the image of the heavenly" (v. 49). We shall wear the image of the heavenly second Adam, whatever his resurrection is like.

(7) In 1 Corinthians 15:50 he contrasts man's fallen condition with his eternal condition in Christ: "Now I say this, brethren, that flesh and blood cannot inherit the kingdom of God; nor does the perishable inherit the imperishable." The phrase "flesh and blood" shows the need for transformation. It highlights the weakened, sinful estate, not the material condition. In the LXX "flesh and blood" stands for human weakness as subject to and indicative of death (cf. Deut 32:42; Isa 49:26; Jer 51:35; Eze 39:17–18; Eph 6:12). Therefore, "flesh and blood" parallels the decayed realm, for "this perishable must put on the imperishable, and this mortal must put on immortality" (1 Cor 15:53). Paul uses *touto* ("this") four times: twice in 53 and twice in 54. His use of "this" demands continuity of the body (this body) even during transformation to the resurrected estate.

Conclusion

When all is said and done, the historic position of orthodox Christianity is sustained. The Hyper-preterist view fails to live up to biblical expectations. Christ is physically resurrected (though with transformed powers) — and so shall we be.

God creates man as distinct from angels. He designs us as *physical* creatures, as we may surmise in that: (1) God sovereignly and purposely creates the objective, material world in which we live (Gen 1; Psa

33:6–11). (2) He lovingly and carefully forms our physical bodies for dwelling in this material world (Gen 2:7–24), which he entrusts to man (Psa 8:1–9; 115:16).

(3) He brings his objective, propositional revelation to us through the historical process of inspiration and inscripturation by means of men moved by the Spirit of God (2 Tim 3:16–17; 2 Pet 1:20–21). (4) In the Second Person of the Trinity, God takes upon himself a true human body and soul (which he still possesses, Col 2:9) and enters history for the purpose of redeeming men back to a right relationship with him (Rom 9:5; Heb 2:14). (5) His elect people will inherit the eternal estate in resurrected, physical bodies (John 5:28–29; 1 Cor 15:20–28) so that we might dwell in a material New Creation order (2 Pet 3:8–13).

Chapter 5
THE TRANSITION TEXT RECOGNIZED

The Olivet Discourse dramatically presents the coming judgment of Israel in AD 70. The first portion of the Discourse focuses on the judgment (Matt 24:1–34) against the temple (Matt 24:1–2) and Israel (24:16). It serves as something of a climactic highpoint in Matthew's Gospel.

Early on in his Gospel Matthew begins pointing to the coming inclusion of the Gentiles in God's plan for history (e.g., Matt 2:2; 8:10–12). And during his ministry Christ himself builds a case against Israel. He shows her unbelief and coming judgment for not being faithful to God's calling (Matt 8:11–12; 10:16–17, 23; 11:20–24; 12:41–42; 23:37–38). Then he finally and climactically presents the Olivet Discourse in his last week of ministry before the cross.

In the Olivet Discourse Jesus also presents material that seems to point beyond Israel's AD 70 holocaust. Clearly the first portion (Matt 24:1–34) is aimed against Israel and her temple (see especially Matt 24:2, 16). But what about the even larger section that remains, Matthew 24:32–25:46? How shall we understand that material? Are the Hyperpreterists correct in seeing the whole of the Discourse as focused on AD 70? I think not.

To properly interpret the Discourse, it is important that we recognize a division in it. I will trace the strong evidence for a dividing line in the Discourse, which separates the AD 70 events from the end-time ones.

The Parable of the Fig Tree

In approaching the latter part of the Discourse we must bear in mind that the disciples originally think that Jesus' prophecy of the destruction of the temple (Matt 24:2) requires the simultaneous conclusion to history. We see this in their question that sparks the Discourse: "as He was sitting on the Mount of Olives, the disciples came to Him privately, saying, 'Tell us, *when* [Gk.: *pote*] will these things be, and *what* [Gk.: *ti*] will be the sign of Your coming, and of the end of the age?'" (24:3).

They were asking *when* the destruction of the temple would occur. And because of their false assumption regarding its permanence they also asked: *what* will be the sign of your coming to effect the end of history?

We must remember that the disciples are often confused at Jesus' teaching.[1]

We see evidence of two questions involved when we carefully analyze the wording of the text. Note their question(s): "Tell us, [1] *when* will these things be, and [2] *what* will be the sign of Your coming, and of the end [*sunteleia*] of the age?" (Matt 24:3). By these "when" and "what" questions they are asking about the *time* of the temple's destruction and the *sign* of his coming—which they believe heralds the temple's end and which they associate with the end of the world.[2] In the Greek only one definite article governs the last phrase: "*the* sign of your coming and end of the age." This shows that this portion of their question really only highlights a single issue, rather than two distinct ones.[3]

As Jews of their day who were proud of their temple (Matt 24:1), the disciples could easily believe that its destruction would herald the end of the world. Hence their linked questions responding to his surprising prophecy. Consider the following evidence in this direction:

First, as just noted, before the outpouring of the Holy Spirit at Pentecost (John 15:26; 16:13; Acts 2:1ff) the disciples are frequently confused about Christ's teaching. For instance, they do not even realize he is going to die and arise again until after these occur (John 20:8–9; cp. 2:22; Matt 28:17). And this is despite his repeatedly teaching them these very things (e.g., Matt 16:21; 20:18). Also some of them continue to hold Zionistic national expectations (Luke 24:21; Acts 1:6), though he resists such (John 6:15) and defines his ministry in contrary terms (John 18:36–37). (He corrects them on these very issues; Luke 24:25; Acts 1:7.)

Second, the disciples undoubtedly imbibed the Jewish conviction that the temple is a permanent institution. For instance, the first-century Jewish philosopher Philo (d. AD 50) wrote regarding the temple's income: "the revenues likewise of the temple will always be preserved, being coeval in their duration with the universal world" (*Spec.* 1:76). In the

---

[1] See: Matt 14:17, 31; 15:15, 33; 16:5–12, 22; 17:10; 18:21; 19:10, 13, 25; 20:24; Acts 11:18.

[2] Matthew uses the word *sunteleia* (which appears in the phrase "the *end* of the age") only for the world's end: Matt 13:39--40, 49; 24:3; 28:20.

[3] Though the phrase "the end of the age" could refer to the end of any particular age (depending on context), Matthew seems to reserve it for the end of history (Matt 13:39–40, 49; 28:20). This "age" refers to history as over against the eternal age (12:32).

Sibylline Oracles (5:400–02) we read that the "temple of God [was] made by holy people and hoped by their soul and body to be always imperishable." Thus, for it to be destroyed must signal the end of history in the eyes of devout Jews.

Third, theologically, a redemptive-historical link does in fact connect AD 70 with the second advent. This could easily confuse the disciples. That is, the AD 70 episode is an anticipatory foreshadowing of the larger event, the second advent. As D. A. Carson expresses it: "The near event, the destruction of Jerusalem, serves as a symbol for the far event," i.e., the second coming."[4] This is akin to there being *several* historical episodes of "the day [singular!] of the Lord" in the Old Testament (Isa 13:6, 9; Eze 13:5; Joel 1:15; 2:1, 11; Amos 5:18, 20; Oba 15; Zeph 1:7; Mal 4:5). Each of these anticipate the final "day of the Lord" event at the end of history (2 Pet 3:10).

Thus, all things in Matthew 24:4–34 (excluding v. 27[5]) — are to occur *in the very generation of the original disciples*: "Truly I say to you, this generation will not pass away until all these things take place." Here in Matthew 24 the phrase "this generation" speaks of the same period as "this generation" in Matthew 23:36. And in Matthew 23 the Lord is rebuking the Scribes and Pharisees *of his own day* (23:13–16, 23, 25, 27, 29). Then in v. 36 he warns them: "I say to you, all these things will come upon this generation." We may not catapult these woes upon the Pharisees to a period two thousand years in the future. Nor should we do so with the "this generation" statement in the next chapter (Matt 24:34).

Here we must remind ourselves that a series of divinely-ordained signs will precede the approaching destruction of the Temple (Matt 24:4ff). The first few signs are general indicators of the final judgment on the Temple: "All these things are merely the beginning of birth pangs" (24:8). All of these signs do, in fact, come to pass in the era before AD 70. And now he informs the disciples that just as surely as fig leaves indicate

---

[4] D. A. Carson, "Matthew," in EBC 12:492.

[5] Matt 24:27 is an aside in the Discourse. Jesus states that when he physically comes again to the earth, it will be an unmistakable event: "For just as the lightning comes from the east, and flashes even to the west, so shall the coming of the Son of Man be" (Matt 24:27). The "for" (*gar*) here shows that he is giving the reason why his disciples should not think he is off in some wilderness or in an inner room somewhere (24:26). After all, when he does return it will be as visible and dramatic as lightning flashing.

approaching summer (24:32), so the events of Matthew 24:4–28 signify the approaching destruction of the temple. But verses 29–31 speak of that event actually coming and of its immediate consequence: the beginning of worldwide redemption.

The Hinge Passage

As Jeffrey Gibbs, R. T. France, and others argue, the Olivet Discourse has a two-part structure which corresponds to the disciples' two questions in Matthew 24:3.[6] Their first question asks "when" the destruction of the temple will occur. This is answered in vv. 4–31. Their second question regards "what" will be sign of "Your coming." This is answered in 24:36–25:46. But how do we *know* this is the intended structure of the passage? It is one thing to *declare* a two-part structure, it is another to *prove* it.

Let us now look at the evidence that Jesus is shifting his attention from the destruction of the temple in AD 70 to his second coming at the end of history. We should keep in mind that AD 70 is theologically linked to the second advent, being a distant picture of it.

1. Argument from concluding statement

By all appearance Matthew 24:34 functions as a *concluding* statement; it seems to *end* the preceding prophecy: "Truly I say to you, this generation will not pass away until all these things take place." Why would such a statement be inserted one-fourth of the way through the discourse if it were dealing *in its entirety* with events that were to occur in "this generation"? Such would not make sense. That would be like someone giving a speech, and after fifteen minutes saying, "In conclusion," then continuing the speech for another forty-five minutes.

In addition, the Lord's very next statement helps confirm our suspicions: "Heaven and earth will pass away, but My words shall not pass away" (Matt 24:35). Here he is confirming his *previous* words. He is declaring *their* certainty: his prophetic words are more sure than even the stability of heaven and earth (cp. Matt 5:18).

Consequently, we must understand Matthew 24:34 as serving to close out one portion of the Discourse. At this point Jesus is announcing that

---

[6] Jeffrey A. Gibbs, *Jerusalem and Parousia: Jesus' Eschatological Discourse in Matthew's Gospel* (St. Louis: Concordia Academic Press, 2000), 167–81. France, *Matthew* (NICNT), 889–96.

he has answered the disciples' question regarding "when" these things shall be (Matt 24:3). He still has their next question before him. This then means that the following material relates to events *not* occurring in "*this generation*." Thus, all prophecies before v. 34 are to transpire within the disciples' own first-century generation.

2. Argument from transition indicator

In Matthew 24:36 we come upon a subject-matter transition device: "*But of* that day and hour no one knows." The introductory phrase here in the Greek is: *peri de* ("but of, concerning, regarding"). This grammatical structure suggests a transition in the passage involving a change of subject.

We see this phrase frequently marking off new material, as in Matthew 22:31; Acts 21:25; 1 Thessalonians 4:9; and 5:1. Allow me to quickly focus on several very clear subject-transition uses of *peri de* in 1 Corinthians. There we see that Paul is turning his attention to one question after another that the Corinthians had asked him: "Now concerning the things about which you wrote" (1 Cor 7:1). "Now concerning virgins" (7:25). "Now concerning things sacrificed to idols" (8:1). "Now concerning spiritual gifts, brethren" (12:1). In each case he is clearly introducing new subjects that respond to different questions presented to him.

Returning to Matthew 24, France notes that v. 36 "marks a deliberate change of subject"[7] Elsewhere he states that it is a "rhetorical formula for a new beginning."[8] John Nolland agrees when he states that *peri de* functions in Matthew 24:36 as "an introductory piece for 24:37–25:30."[9]

What is more, Gibbs demonstrates that the lone preposition *peri* can in and of itself have a resumptive force.[10] That is, *peri* ("concerning") can pick up on a subject broached earlier in a narrative by serving as a sign that the speaker is returning to that issue once again. Gibbs offers two illustrations from Matthew's Gospel, one from Matthew 6:25 and the other from Matthew 22:23ff.

In Matthew 6:25 Jesus challenges his followers not to be anxious regarding *both* "what you shall eat" (food) *and* "what you shall put on"

---

[7] R. T. France, *Matthew* (TNTC) (Downers Grove, Ill.: InterVarsity, 1985), 347.

[8] France, *Matthew* (NICNT), 936.

[9] John Nolland, *The Gospel of Matthew* (NIGTC) (Grand Rapids: Eerdmans, 2005), 990.

[10] Gibbs, *Jerusalem and Parousia*, 172.

(clothing). Then in v. 26 he immediately urges them to "look at the birds" to observe that "your heavenly Father feeds them." He intends this to resolve their first anxiety regarding food. Then in v. 28 he returns to his original exhortation in v. 25 and picks up on their second concern, *clothing*: "And why [*kai peri*] are you anxious about clothing?" (6:28). Thus, his instruction in verses 28 and 29 picks up on a portion of his earlier statement in v. 25; it *resumes* his initial concern regarding clothing.

The same function operates in Matthew 22. In Matthew 22:23–28 the Sadducees "came to Him and questioned Him" about the resurrection, giving a hypothetical example of a man who was married seven times. In vv. 29–30 Jesus deals with their example, then in v. 31 he reaches back to their original question about the resurrection and states: "but regarding [*peri de*] the resurrection of the dead, have you not read...?" Once again we see the resumptive force of the preposition *peri*.

So now for our purposes: in Matthew 24:36 *peri* reaches back to the disciples' *second* question of the two that were raised in v. 3. Having dealt with their *first* question in vv. 4–35, he now returns to consider their second one. By this structuring of the passage we see that v. 36 introduces new material differing from vv. 4–35. At this point he moves away from his AD 70 prophecy and begins speaking of his second advent at the "end of the age," which he will cover in 24:36–25:46.

3. Argument from humiliation limitation

Focusing once again on Matthew 24:36 we read: "But of that day and hour no one knows, not even the angels of heaven, *nor the Son*, but the Father alone." Here Christ declares that in his state of humiliation (the period from the time of his earthly conception within Mary's womb until his glorification at his resurrection) he himself has no knowledge as to when "that day and hour" will occur. But of what "day and hour" is he speaking?

He must be speaking of his future second advent because, in the preceding section of his Discourse, he informs his disciples of numerous signs, noting that "the end [of the temple] is not yet" (Matt 24:6). This indicates that he definitely knows when *that* event will occur. He also dogmatically teaches them that these earlier things will certainly happen in "this generation" (24:34). Thus, as John Nolland notes: "there is a deliberate contrast between the confident tone of the predictive materials thus far in the chapter, climaxing in v. 34, and the present insistence that only the Father knows."[11]

4. Argument from temporal markers

As we continue looking at Matthew 24:36 we also note that it lacks any temporal-transition markers to link it with the preceding events. It is wholly unconnected with the preceding material in terms of temporal progression. This is surprising in that in the preceding material we see a well-connected historical progress with recurring "then" statements (24:9, 14, 16, 21, 23, 30), as well as an "immediately after" (24:29) declaration.

But when Christ makes the statement in Matthew 24:36 we hear nothing that links it with the preceding material. We hear absolutely no "then" or "after" nor any other such temporal progress indicator. Thus, as France notes: "its contents stand apart from the historical sequence hitherto described."[12] This is because it is distantly separated from the events of AD 70 (see numbers 5 and 13 below where he contrasts near events with distant ones).

5. Argument from demonstrative distinction

In Matthew 24:34–36 provides further evidence of a subject transition. Jesus contrasts near and far events:

> "Truly I say to you, *this* generation will not pass away until all *these* things take place." (Matt 24:34)
>
> "But of *that* day and hour no one knows, not even the angels of heaven, nor the Son, but the Father alone." (Matt 24:36)

In this passage "*this* generation" is set in contrast to "*that* day."

With these words the Lord looks beyond the signs just given for "this [*haute*] generation" (Matt 24:34) to the event of "that [*ekeines*] day" (24:36). According to BAGD (740 under *houtos*): the word *haute* is a "demonstrative pron[oun], used as adj[ective] and subst[antive]," and can point to a "person or thing comparatively near at hand in the discourse material, *this, this one* (contrast *ekeinos* referring to someth[ing] comparatively farther away' cp. Lk 18:14; Js 4:15)." Thus, the Lord's attention turns to his distant second advent at the end of history.

---

[11] Nolland, *Matthew*, 991.

[12] France, *Matthew* (NICNT), 983.

6. Argument from observational prospects

Before his statement in Matthew 24:34, Christ mentions numerous events that serve as historical signs, events such as: "wars and rumors of wars" (Matt 24:6), "famines and earthquakes" (v. 7), "false prophets" (v. 11), and so forth. He specifically mentions a pre-eminent sign: "the sign of the Son of Man."

Furthermore, he personalizes this portion of his Discourse by repeatedly warning the very disciples sitting before him on the Mount of Olives (Matt 24:3):

"see to it that no one misleads *you*" (Matt 24:4)
"*you* will be hearing of wars" (v. 6a)
"see that *you* are not frightened" (v. 6b)
"they will deliver *you* to tribulation, and will kill *you*" (v. 9)
"when *you* see the Abomination of Desolation" (v. 15)
"if anyone says to *you*" (v. 23)
"behold, I have told *you* in advance" (v. 25)
"if therefore they say to *you*" (v. 26)
"*you* too, when *you* see all these things" (v. 33)

Thus, he is informing his disciples (who asked him the questions) how *they* might know the time of the coming end of the temple; it is a predictable event.

In fact, the Lord even gives the disciples a parable illustrating how the event coming in their lifetimes can be known, urging them to properly read all the signs:

> "Now learn the parable from the fig tree: when its branch has already become tender, and puts forth its leaves, you know that summer is near; even so you too, when you see all these things, recognize that He is near, right at the door." (Matt 24:32–33)

But after Matthew 24:34 Jesus drops all mention of signs and predictability. Instead he includes statements emphasizing absolute surprise and total unpredictability:

"But of that day and hour no one knows, not even the angels of heaven, nor the Son, but the Father alone" (24:36)
"they did not understand" (v. 39)
"you do not know" (v. 42)
"if the head of the house had known" (v. 43)
"coming at an hour when you do not think He will" (v. 44)
"he does not expect him" (v. 50)
"you do not know" (25:13)

This indicates that the following section involves an event that is coming at an altogether unknown and indeterminable time. He is no longer speaking of the destruction of the temple in AD 70, but of his second coming in the distant future.

7. Argument from multiple days

By the very nature of the case, the numerous events leading up to the Roman military destruction of the temple in AD 70 will require a number of days. Hence, in the portion of his Discourse prior to Matthew 24:36 Jesus mentions "those *days* [plural]" (vv. 19, 29) and even comforts his disciples by noting that "those *days*" will be "cut short" (v. 22).

This mention of the *days* of the tribulation period are set in stark contrast to the singular *day* — indeed, the exact moment — of the second coming: "But of that *day* and *hour* no one knows, not even the angels of heaven, nor the Son, but the Father alone" (Matt 24:36). After this transition at 24:36 he repeatedly mentions the singular "day" (24:42, 50) or "the day" and "the hour" (25:13). The second advent does not involve a series of historical actions, as is the case with the Roman military operations against the Jews, Jerusalem, and the temple. The second advent is a one-time, catastrophic event conducted by a singular individual, Christ himself.

8. Argument from deception fears

In the first part of the Discourse Jesus repeatedly warns of the danger of deception by those who would "mislead" (*planao*) :

> "And Jesus answered and said to them, 'See to it that no one misleads you. For many will come in My name, saying, "I am the Christ," and will mislead many."' (Matt 24:4–5)
>
> "And many false prophets will arise, and will mislead many." (24:11)
>
> "For false Christs and false prophets will arise and will show great signs and wonders, so as to mislead, if possible, even the elect." (24:24)

Furthermore, we should note that he even mentions deception caused by false Christs (Matt 24:5, 23–27) and false prophets (24:11, 24). The false Christs will deceive many by claiming to be Christ himself (24:5), while many people will claim that Christ is here or there (24:23).

Indeed, the Lord warns that these are obvious deceivers because when he returns in his second advent, it will be impossible to miss; no deception will be possible: "For just as the lightning comes from the east, and flashes even to the west, so shall the coming of the Son of Man be" (Matt 24:27).

All of this serves as a significant indicator of a subject shift when we compare this to his teaching after Matthew 24:36. After that point he no longer mentions the danger of deceit: the word *planao* ("mislead") vanishes from the narrative. In fact, the second advent will suddenly overwhelm people in the midst of their daily activities: they will be eating, and drinking and marrying (Matt 24:38–39). They will be working in the field (v. 40). They will be grinding at the mill (v. 41). They will be as surprised as one whose house is broken into without warning (v. 43).

Contrary to this, no one would be surprised at the destruction of the temple in AD 70. After all, the Romans took five months of relentless siege warfare to get into Jerusalem and destroy the temple after they encircled Jerusalem in April, AD 70. And even this occurs well after the formal engagement of the Jewish War in the Spring of AD 67 and the early military operations in Galilee and elsewhere.

9. Argument from social contrasts

The social circumstances of the early portion of the Olivet Discourse dramatically differ from those of the latter portion. In the first section (up to Matt 24:36) all is chaotic, dangerous, and confused. This period is laden with wars and rumors of wars (Matt 24:6–7), famines and earthquakes (v. 7), betrayal and persecution (v. 10), lawlessness (v. 12), and great tribulation (v. 21). Thus, woe upon woe befalls men in the chaotic first portion of the Discourse.

But in the second section all of this upheaval and danger disappears. Social activities appear tranquil, allowing business as usual while the mundane activities of life continue. People are marrying and eating and drinking (Matt 24:38), working in the field (v. 40), and grinding at the mill (v. 41). The wholesale chaos leading up to AD 70 stands in stark contrast to the peaceable conditions at the time of Christ's second coming.

10. Argument from flight opportunity

In the first section Christ urges desperate flight from the area, clearly implying there will be time and opportunity to flee: "then let those who are in Judea flee to the mountains" (Matt 24:16). In fact, one particular sign — the abomination of desolation — will be the cue to leave the area. Because of this opportunity of flight, many lives of God's elect will be saved: "unless those days had been cut short, no life would have been saved; but for the sake of the elect those days shall be cut short" (24:22).

But upon entering the second section of the Discourse we hear of no commands to escape, no opportunities for flight. Indeed, we witness just the opposite. Once again we can read through the warnings of the unpredictable nature of the second advent (as in # 6 above) and realize that by the very nature of the case no opportunity for flight will exist:

> "But of that day and hour no one knows, not even the angels of heaven, nor the Son, but the Father alone" (24:36)
> "they did not understand" (v. 39)
> "you do not know" (v. 42)
> "if the head of the house had known" (v. 43)
> "coming at an hour when you do not think He will" (v. 44)
> "he does not expect him" (v. 50)
> "you do not know" (25:13)

11. Argument from narrative function

Gibbs notes that when we compare the two sections of the Lord's Olivet Discourse we may quickly observe that the first section issues *warnings* regarding deception and danger.[13] For instance, we hear: "see to it that no one misleads you" (Matt 24:4); "you will be hearing of wars" (24:6); "they will deliver you to tribulation, and will kill you" (24:9); and so forth.

The second section of the narrative differs in tone by issuing *exhortations* related to future judgment and reward, calling upon the reader to exercise faithfulness and diligence. The reader is exhorted to "be on the alert" (Matt 24:42); to "be ready" (24:44), with the result that he will be considered "the faithful and sensible slave" (24:45).

Jesus also gives a parable contrasting the foolish and the prudent (Matt 25:1–12) which ends with an exhortation to "be on the alert then" (25:13). In addition he presents a parable on the trustworthy and the untrustworthy slaves (25:14– 30). The slaves who invest for the future are each commended as being "a good and faithful slave" (25:21, 23).

Then in Matthew 25:31–46 the Lord speaks of the final judgment "when the Son of Man comes in His glory, and all the angels with Him" (Matt 25:31a). Here he "separates the sheep from the goats" (25:32b) based on the evidence of their true conversion exhibited by their love for Christ and his people (25:35–46). Thus, he so frames the final judgment that it serves as an exhortation to continuance in the faith and among God's people.

Fearful warnings of imminent danger in the earlier section greatly differ from moral exhortations to long-term faithfulness and preparedness

---

[13] Gibbs, *Jerusalem and Parousia*, 172.

in the latter section. This difference demonstrates what we have seen on the basis of other considerations, that is, that these two sections are fundamentally different.

12. Argument from eschatological contrast

Jesus appears to use key terms that distinguish his metaphorical coming in AD 70 from his literal coming at the second advent. In Matthew 24:4–34 he never uses the word *parousia* ("coming," "presence") — except in v. 27 where he intentionally distinguishes his visible second advent from the first-century (24:34) deceptions which claim Jesus is hidden here or there (24:24–26).

This is significant in that the disciples' original question regarding his "coming" uses the word *parousia*: "what will be the sign of Your coming [*parousia*]" (Matt 24:3). Yet Jesus studiously avoids the term to describe events occurring in the first section, though he does use the word *erchomenos* ("coming") in the key verse at 24:30: "then the sign of the Son of Man will appear in the sky, and then all the tribes of the earth will mourn, and they will see the Son of Man coming [*erchomenos*] on the clouds of the sky with power and great glory."

After Matthew 24:34, though, he twice uses *parousia* of that unpredictable coming in the distant future:

> "For the coming [*parousia*] of the Son of Man will be just like the days of Noah." (24:37)
>
> "They did not understand until the flood came and took them all away; so shall the coming [*parousia*] of the Son of Man be." (v. 39)

And just to make the evidence a "Baker's dozen," I will conclude with:

13. Argument from temporal duration

In the early section of Matthew 24, the time frame is short. The disciples will be facing real dangers that will transpire in "this generation" (Matt 24:34). They are to be on the lookout for various signs, especially that one that occurs within the then-standing temple (24:15), for then they are to flee the area (24:16). This all fits with Jesus' introductory warning of the judgment that will befall the scribes and Pharisees — which will also be in "this generation" (23:34–36).

In the following section from Matthew 24:36 and into chapter 25, the time frame is much longer. No longer do we hear of "this generation," rather Jesus' parables anticipate a distant future:

> "But if that evil servant says in his heart, 'My master is *delaying* his coming.'" (Matt 24:48)

"But while the bridegroom was *delayed*, they all slumbered and slept." (Matt 25:5)

"After a *long time* the lord of those servants came and settled accounts with them." (Matt 25:19)

Conclusion

Although the Olivet Discourse is an important passage for demonstrating the preterist analysis, it is wrongly used by Hyper-preterists who apply the entire Discourse to AD 70. A careful analysis of its setting and grammar provides strong evidence that the Lord established a transition passage in Matthew 24:34–36. This transition passage allows both preterist analysis of AD 70 and affirms the orthodox view of the future return of Christ. The two judgment events are linked: one presages the other.

Chapter 6
THE CREEDAL DENIAL CRITIQUED[1]

Introduction

Christianity is an historical religion created by a supernatural faith. The living Church must remain steadfast in her historical faith despite all the challenges she will face on earth. And though many verses also hold out the promise of victory, Warfield has perceptively observed: "the chief dangers to Christianity do not come from the anti-Christian systems.... It is corrupt forms of Christianity itself which menace from time to time the life of Christianity."[2]

Consequently, as the church weathers the lightning storms of external opposition and the howling winds of internal corruption while she sails forward through time, she must appreciate her creedal past as "the ballast that will steady [her] in the storms of the present."[3]

My creedal concern

This book is critiquing Hyper-preterism, a corrosive theological fad that is seeping into evangelical and conservative churches. In this chapter I will be presenting an historical argument against its views: I will present the argument from the historic creeds of the church. I do this in order to establish the significance of the debate. I am defending the historic, corporate, public, universal, systematic Christian faith. I do so against the eroding forces of novelty flowing from the tributaries of historical confusion, exegetical failure, theological naivete, and logical fallacies.

The creedal argument is important, not as the *final* word in the debate but as a *crucial* concern. I reflect upon the creedal question because of my

---

[1] This chapter was originally published in Keith L. Mathison, ed., *When Shall These Things Be?* as Chapter 1: "The Historical Problem of Hyper-Preterism" by Kenneth L Gentry Jr. (ISBN 978-0-87552-552-5). This book was published by P&R Publishing Co., P.O. Box 817, Phillipsburg, N.J. 08865 copyright 2004. The material has been slightly edited to fit the current book.

[2] B. B. Warfield, *Selected Shorter Writings of Benjamin B. Warfield* (Phillipsburg, N.J.: P & R, rep. 1973), 2:665-66.

[3] David F. Wells, *No Place for Truth: Or Whatever Happened to Evangelical Theology?* (Grand Rapids: Eerdmans, 1993), 100.

desire to promote the "universal doctrine" of the church, the "heritage of the church," the "second pillar" of evangelical theology, "the historical tradition of the one true church."[4] I humbly do this over against innovation, experimentation, and obfuscation in theological pursuits. Creeds represent "the public doctrinal inheritance of the Christian tradition."[5]

Hyper-preterism has arisen among Christians (largely from within the Church of Christ sect) who express little interest in the creedal integrity of the historic Christian faith. One leading proponent of the Hyper-preterist movement states this concern: "Is it safe to assume that the early church understood all doctrinal matters so clearly that no mistakes were possible?"[6] In the same article he eventually declares (on his own recognizance): "I believe the time has come for the creeds to be revised."

My preterist concern

I have a deep interest in promoting a preterist understanding of various New Testament prophecies. Unfortunately though, the rise of Hyper-preterism has caused me much concern: I have seen immature Christians swallow the system whole, then become intoxicated with a cult-like arrogance. I have had many pastors call me for counsel on how to deal with combative Hyper-preterist zealots entering their congregations and disrupting the unity and peace of the church. I have had ministerial friends forsake their orthodox preterism because of the fear of being confused with the extremists. I have read scathing reviews of Hyper-preterist materials that heap scorn upon any preterist approach.[7] I have witnessed Hyper-preterists causing concerns due to their obsessive single-mindedness.

For instance, conference organizers at Ligonier's 1999 National Conference on Eschatology were forced to pull aside Hyper-preterists

---

[4] Stanley J. Grenz, *Revisioning Evangelical Theology* (Downers Grove, Ill.: InterVarsity, 1993), 97, 105.

[5] Stephen Sykes, *The Identity of Christianity: Theologians and the Essence of Christianity from Schleiermacher to Barth* (Philadelphia: Fortress, 1984). Cited from Wells, *No Place for Truth*, 99.

[6] Edward E. Stevens, "What If the Creeds are Wrong?" International Preterist Association internet paper.

[7] A. Boyd Luter, Review of *Beyond the End Times: The Rest of the Greatest Story Ever Told*. By John Noe *Journal of the Evangelical Theological Society* 43:4 (December 2000): 743-744.

bedecked with promotional tee-shirt logos in order to direct them to cease-and-desist from "proselytizing" conferees with their missionary zeal. At a conference engagement in April 2002, I spoke briefly with a leader in the movement who came to the conference wearing a shirt monogrammed with the statement: "Preterism's Pit Bull." An unusual illustration of the one-track mindedness of Hyper-preterist enthusiasts is provided by Jim West in his Chalcedon website article: "The Allurement of Hymenaen Preterism: The Rise of 'Dispensable Eschatology.'" West noted that a visitor to a fellow pastor's church signed the guest register then wrote after his name: "preterist."

And more personally, in 1997 I was subjected to a withering presbytery exam that (in part) attempted to equate my historic preterism with Hyper-preterism.[8] I have endured a steady flow of e-mail challenges from Hyper-preterists because of my disagreement with their views. I have weathered logically confused, excruciatingly redundant, physically wearisome responses to my writings from Hyper-preterist theologues.[9]

Hyper-preterism is a small but active, militant, and widely-spread heterodox theological movement. Its enthusiastic adherents loudly demand that those who disagree with them stop their full-time labors and deal with all their questions — or die the death of a thousand e-mails.[10]

One serious problem with the movement as such — besides its zealotry and combativeness — is its naivete. The Foreword to a Hyper-preterist book by John Noe inadvertently highlights the (all too typical) problem: "John is not a professional theologian. He has had no formal seminary training, but that may be an advantage."[11] Then again, lacking formal training in biblical languages, exegetical principles, systematic

---

[8] Some Christian scholars quickly write off preterism altogether — because of the extravagances of Hyper-preterism, e.g., Robert L. Reymond, *A New Systematic Theology of the Christian Faith* (Nashville: Thomas Nelson, 1998), 1067-68.

[9] One five page pamphlet I wrote was titled *A Brief Theological Analysis of Hyper-preterism* (1995). It has generated scores of "rebuttals," one of which runs around 160 pages.

[10] I once facetiously warned Andrew Sandlin, editor of *The Chalcedon Report*, to be cautious in responding to the Hyper-preterists because they are unemployed and have Internet access. After he published his article, he wrote me within a week and said he discovered what I meant.

[11] John Noe, *Beyond the End Times: The Rest of ... the Greatest Story Ever Told* (Bradford, Penn.: Preterist Resources, 1999), x.

theology, and church history may not be helpful to biblical interpretation at all. The scathing review I mentioned previously noted that "one of the intriguing theological trends of the last decade or so has been the role of theological laymen in plotting out and popularizing eschatological systems."[12]

My chapter approach

Space limitations prohibit any complete survey of the great body of the Hyper-preterists' published writings (most of which are Internet postings), as well as any thorough analysis of even a few particular studies. To reduce the project to manageable proportions, I will focus primarily (though not exclusively) on the creedal comments found in studies by Edward E. Stevens. I do this for several reasons:

Stevens (1) is recognized as a leader of one of the larger factions in this movement, (2) is the founder of the International Preterist Association, (3) hosts one of the most significant Hyper-preterism websites (www.preterist.org), (4) has written voluminously on the topic, (5) has specifically responded at length to my objection to the anti-creedal nature of his theology,[13] and (6) even claims to have "embraced Reformed covenant theology."[14]

I will use the following abbreviations to refer to various articles from Stevens' website and from his printed materials. Please note that the website articles have no pagination available:

CPO Stevens: "Creeds and Preterist Orthodoxy" (web article)
RGA Stevens: "Response to Gentry's Analysis of the Full Preterist View" (web article)
WH Stevens: *What Happened in A. D. 70?* (5th. ed.: Bradford, Penn.: Kingdom Publications, 1997)
WICW Stevens: "What If the Creeds Are Wrong?" (web article)

---

[12] Luter, Review of *Beyond the End Times*, 744. Dispensationalism is replete with such: Dave Hunt is a trained accountant; Tim LaHaye is a professional counsellor.

[13] Edward E. Stevens, "Response to Gentry's Analysis of the Full Preterist View" (hereinafter RGA).

[14] Edward E. Stevens, *What Happened in A. D. 70?* (5th. ed.: Bradford, Penn.: Kingdom Publications, 1997), vi (hereinafter WH). Elsewhere he states: "It is especially important for all of us in the Reformed tradition...." Foreword to John Noe, *Beyond the End Times*, x.

I will also refer to other Hyper-preterist materials from time to time, using the following abbreviations:

- BET John Noe: *Beyond the End Times: The Rest of… the Greatest Story Ever Told* (Bradford, Penn.: Preterist Resources, 1999).
- DAIS J. E. Gautier, "Do As I Say, Not As I Do" (web article)
- PA J. E. Gautier, "Preterist Apologetic" (web article)
- PEC David A. Green: "Preterism and the Ecumenical Creeds" (web article)
- WHH Daniel E. Harden: "When Is a Heretic Not a Heretic"? (web article)

Dangers of Hyper-preterism

One of the glories of Christian doctrine is its systemic consistency. McGrath notes that "doctrines are not stated or developed in isolation. They interact with one another. Rightly understood there is a wonderful coherence to Christian doctrine."[15] Van Til stresses the inter-dependence of doctrine thus: "A truly Protestant method of reasoning involves a stress upon the fact that the meaning of every aspect or part of Christian theism depends upon Christian theism as a unit."[16]

Unfortunately, this internal coherence can also serve as a slippery slope to grave theological error. That is, when serious error arises in one area of doctrine, it can easily and quickly topple over into other areas. We are already witnessing this in Hyper-preterism as it shakes itself free of all creedal constraints.

Hyper-preterism's methodological relativism

Hyper-preterism is an extremist eschatology that undercuts the well-established, centuries-old, universally-affirmed theological foundations of Christian theology. In an effort to operate within orthodox churches (their second leading mission field after the Internet), Hyper-preterists urge the well-known humanist shibboleth of *tolerance*. To secure their place in the church, they urge a dangerous latitudinarianism, a theological relativism.[17]

---

[15] Alister E. McGrath, *Studies in Doctrine* (Grand Rapids: Zondervan, 1997), 309.

[16] Cornelius Van Til, *An Introduction to Systematic Theology* (Phillipsburg, N.J.: P & R, 1974), 239.

[17] For the dangers of latitudinarianism see Warfield, *Selected Shorter Writings*, 2:15ff: "The Right of Systematic Theology." See also: John Murray, *Collected Writings of John Murray* (Edinburgh: Banner of Truth, 1982), 1:273-79: "Corporate

Stevens complains about the "dangers of using our creedalized opinions for defining our circles of fellowship" (WICW). He criticizes concern for doctrinal fidelity as a form of spiritual immaturity: "Too many Christians just have not matured to the point of allowing and tolerating of opinions" (CPO). His view of Christian unity elevates attitude over doctrine: "Unity is not so much agreement to a list of doctrines (a creed), but rather an attitude of charity (agreeableness) and tolerance which gives freedom to differ without making a test of fellowship over it" (CPO). Indeed, in our theological debate he calls for "tolerance and openness toward each other's beliefs" (WICW).

In decrying doctrinally-rooted unity Stevens even goes so far as to argue that "it is not extreme opinions that disrupt unity as much as it is the exclusive way those opinions are pushed. Extreme views are much more likely to be tolerated if those who hold them are tolerant of each other" (CPO). Given today's doctrinal declension he is probably correct: a bright smile and a warm handshake mean much more than doctrinal integrity.[18]

Not only does Stevens urge an attitudinal over against a doctrinal basis for ecclesiastical acceptance and cooperation, but such tolerance will inevitably lead to theological relativism. In fact, Stevens expressly states that we can never be certain that Christianity has the truth: "As the centuries unfold and our understanding of the Bible gets better, more and more defects in the creeds will start showing up, as is beginning to happen now with the preterist [*sc.* Hyper-preterist] view" (WICW). Why? Because creeds "are a snapshot of what the saints believed and understood at a particular time and place in history" (WICW). "The creeds embodied the best understanding and interpretation of Biblical truth that they were able to arrive at in the day" (WICW).

This is precisely the view of nineteenth century liberalism in its opposition to creedal orthodoxy, for, as Hatch notes, "theological liberals became increasingly restive with strict creedal definitions of Christ-

---

Responsibility"; 1:280-87: "The Creedal Basis of Union in the Church."

[18] For the problem of doctrinal confusion and decline see: Wells, *No Place for Truth* and Michael S. Horton, ed., *Agony of Deceit* (Chicago: Moody, 1990). Andrew Sandlin, *Keeping Our Sacred Trust: Biblical Authority, Creedal Orthodoxy, and Heresy* (Vallecito, Calif.: Chalcedon, 1999).

ianity."[19] In fact, it parallels almost exactly the Unitarian rejection of creeds: "What Unitarians object to in these or other creeds is the implied intention to bind future generations to the ideas, insights, and literal words of the past. It may well be that the Apostles' Creed or the Nicene Creed were good and accurate formulations of the beliefs of most Christians in the third and fourth centuries. But we see no reason why they should remain definitive for religious persons in all times."[20]

Thus, even after 2000 years the church cannot hope to proclaim anything more than a message that is potentially defective at its root. Stevens even leaves cardinal truths regarding *salvation* exposed to the ravages of time: "Even in this area of 'essentials for salvation' we must consider the possibility that we have misunderstood some things" (WICW). He warns: "Why shouldn't creeds be used to test orthodoxy? Because we can never be sure the creeds themselves are orthodox" (WICW). In effect, we must adopt the humanist principle that nothing is certain but change: "A better understanding will constantly be developed" (CPO).

This is the bitter fruit of anti-creedalism. And such fruit is poisonous. Its danger becomes all the more glaringly evident as we realize the theological naivete of its proponents, a naivete not unlike the Jehovah's Witnesses that knock on our doors. This theological posturing parallels the Auburn Affirmation which encouraged Presbyterian church courts in "accepting theological differences within its bounds and subordinating them to recognized loyalty to Jesus Christ and united work for the kingdom of God."[21] The tolerance principle has even been urged by theological liberals to welcome Mormons to the Christian community of ideas because "the old symbolisms, the clichés, the ancient shibboleths

---

[19] Nathan Hatch, "Sola Scriptura and Novus Ordo Seclorum," in Nathan Hatch and Mark Noll, eds., *The Bible in America: Essays in Cultural History* (New York: Oxford University Press, 1982), 63. As cited in Andrew Sandlin, *Keeping Our Sacred Trust: Biblical Authority, Creedal Orthodoxy, and Heresy* (Vallecito, Calif.: Chalcedon, 1999), 164.

[20] Harry C. Meserve, "Religion Without Dogma," in Harry B. Scholefield, ed., *A Pocket Guide to Unitarianism* (Boston: Beacon, 1954), 1.

[21] Philip W. Butin, "Auburn Affirmation," in *ERP*, 17.

out of which the meaning has gone, are irrelevant."[22] The doctrinal future does not bode well for Hyper-preterists.

Hyper-preterism's cultic tendencies

As Samuel Miller (1769-1850) perceptively observed: "the most ardent and noisy opponents of creeds have been those who held corrupt opinions."[23] Philip Schaff (1819–93) noted the same tendency: "The heretical sects connected with Protestantism mostly reject symbolical books altogether, as a yoke of human authority and a new kind of popery."[24] An old adage declares: "Men are seldom opposed to creeds, until creeds have become opposed to them."

Breaking with historic Christian doctrine is a necessary starting point for cultic aberrations. For instance, Joseph Smith claimed that God revealed to him that he should not join any church for "they were all wrong — their creeds were an abomination in his sight; ... they teach for doctrines the commandments of men."[25] Below I will highlight a few danger signals that may suggest we are witnessing the sprouting of a new unorthodox sect that could eventually blossom into a full-fledged cult. As a matter of fact, Stevens threatens: "If we are forced out of present groups, then there is no recourse but to form new ones" (CPO). Indeed, some churches have organized themselves around Hyper-preterist principles, and are now untethered from the wider Christian community.[26]

One Hyper-preterist has proudly written:

> "In many respects Preterists are the first fruits of the emerging church. The honour and the responsibility of preparing the way for the rest to follow is ours. The many contributors to this and other Preterist sites reveal that God has appointed a smart and willing team of labourers. It

---

[22] Marcus Bock, "Review of C. S. Braden, *These Also Believe* in *The Christian Century* (July 6, 1949). Cited in Jan Karel Van Baalen, *The Chaos of Cults: A Study in Present-day Isms* (Rev. ed.: Grand Rapids: Eerdmans, 1956), 385.

[23] Samuel Miller, *Doctrinal Integrity: The Utility and Importance of Creeds and Confessions and Adherence to Our Doctrinal Standards* (Dallas, Tex.: Presbyterian Heritage, rep. 1841), 24.

[24] Philip Schaff, *The Creeds of Christendom: With a History and Critical Notes*, 6th ed., ed. David S. Schaff, vol. 1, (New York: Harper and Row, 1931; reprint, Grand Rapids: Baker, 1990), 11.

[25] Melvin Brooks, *LDS Encyclopedia* (Salt Lake City: Bookcraft, 1960), 73.

[26] See the testimony, for example, on the Preterist Archive website: David B. Curtis, "The Birth of a Preterist Church."

is encumbent upon us to do the work today to prepare the church for tomorrow. Futurists often run from Preterism simply because they have never planned for the future. They have no working models. God is calling us to begin to develop those models."[27]

Creedal resistance

Since this chapter is focusing on the question of creedal symbols, I should note anti-creedal parallels between known cults and Hyper-preterism. For instance, Mormons promote their corporeal conception of God as a return to original Christianity and away from the creeds. Introducing the Nicene Creed, James Talmage explains: "The consistent, simple, and authentic doctrine respecting the character and attributes of God, such as was taught by Christ and the apostles, gave way as revelation ceased and as the darkness incident to the absence of divine authority fell upon the world.... And in its place appeared numerous theories and dogmas of men."[28]

Similarly, a Mormon hierarch complains: "By the 4th century formal doctrines called *creeds* had been formulated, adopted by councils, and the dogmas expressed in them imposed upon the church.... Eventually they became the accepted standards and guides in religious matters. They are considered authoritative declarations of belief.... The most charitable thing that can be said of them is that they are man made."[29] Another Mormon leaders states: "The creeds of apostate Christendom teach untruths."[30] Joseph Smith himself stated: "*The creeds set up stakes*, and say, 'Hitherto shalt thou come, and no further,' which I cannot subscribe to."[31]

In citing an episode in the ministry of Christ that is a favorite of Hyper-preterists (Matt 15:2-14; Mark 7:2-13), Jehovah's Witnesses complain about creeds: "Such traditions men have since recorded and published as being equal to the inspired Scriptures or even superior to the

---

[27] Albert Persohn, "It's the Church Stupid!" (www.planetpreterist.com article).

[28] James E. Talmage, *A Study of the Articles of Faith: Being a Consideration of the Principal Doctrines of The Church of Jesus Christ of Latter-day Saints* (Salt Lake City: Deseret, rep. 1984 [1913]), 42-43.

[29] Cited in Bruce R. McConkie, *Mormon Doctrine* (Salt Lake City: Bookcraft, 1966), 170-71.

[30] McConkie, *Mormon Doctrine*, 440.

[31] Cited in McConkie, *Mormon Doctrine*, 171.

Scripture where there is a conflict between the two."[32] Elsewhere they urge: "We need to examine, not only what we personally believe, but also what is taught by any religious organization with which we may be associated. Are its teachings in full harmony with God's Word, or are they based on the traditions of men."[33]

Sounding very like the Jehovah's Witness publication title *Let God Be True*, Stevens urges: "Let God through His Word (not the creeds) be the judge" (WICW). Noe challenges us: "Whom should we believe? Jesus and the inspired writers of Scripture, or the uninspired framers of the creeds? Elevating these man-made doctrines to too lofty a position puts us in danger of continuing the same sin for which Jesus condemned the Pharisees and scribes" (then he cites Mark 7:8-13) (BET 215).

Noe even condescendingly dismisses the second advent by prefacing a statement regarding it with these words: "Traditionalists assure us that..." (BET 113). He challenges his followers to exercise due courage in resisting the traditional, orthodox doctrine of the church and her creeds: "let's not be intimidated or brainwashed by the traditions of men" (BET 205).

Hyper-preterist Green admits that "some preterists" are so opposed to the creeds that they dismiss the "institutional church": "since the creeds were written by, and have been endorsed by, the 'institutional church,' ... there is no reason to presume that the true Gospel ever found its way into the creeds" (PEC).

In a testimony regarding a local church split over the matter, a Hyper-preterist pastor defensively writes: "Let me just say here that we didn't resign over *eschatology*, we resigned over the reformation principle of 'Sola Scriptura!' The Scripture alone. It doesn't matter what men's doctrinal statements say, or what church tradition says, what needs to be the guiding principle of our lives is: What does the Scripture say?"[34] Thus, it becomes this pastor v. the historic Christian interpretation.

Stevens proudly sets himself against the historic church: "I am surprised at Gentry's hesitancy to believe the historical church could have missed a few things" (RGA). He contends that "full preterists are Reformers, and as such it should be obvious that we believe the early

---

[32] *Let God Be True* (New York: Watchtower, 1946), 12.

[33] *The Truth That Leads to Eternal Life* (New York: Watchtower, 1968), 13.

[34] David B. Curtis, "The Birth of a Preterist Church." Web article from Preteristarchive.com.

church and the creeds can be (and have been found to be) mistaken" (RGA). He even writes as if centuries of Bible study had been gradually building the case for Hyper-preterist conclusions: "Centuries of further Bible study reveals that there are some problems in our 'interpretations and applications' of Scripture" regarding the creeds and the Second Advent (RGA).[35]

Stevens is confident that he and his followers have finally resolved the eschatological "problem" that eluded the universal, historic Christian church: "Is it possible that a mistake could have occurred very early in the formative period of the creeds and have gotten perpetuated down through centuries until finally noted by later Christians who understand Scripture better" (WICW).[36]

Zealous calls to follow

With a tone and zeal familiar from cultic circles, Stevens writes in an e-mail dated February 6, 2002:

> "Only the Preterist view has the Biblical viscerals to do the job of reform that is needed. The sooner we 'always reforming' guys realize that and tap into it, the better. Why piddle around in a '3 or 4 point' partial preterism the rest of your life and miss out on the chance to be a leader in the next big wave of reform that is about to sweep over the Christians landscape? The Preterist movement is where the next BIG reformation is going to come form, since ONLY a fully consistent preterist approach to scripture will provide an irresistible and unconquerable WORLDVIEW with which to shape 'all generations of the ages of the ages' to come. The partial preterist worldview just won't cut it, even though it is admittedly a step in the right direction, and far better than what we had in past generations. But it doesn't hold a candle to the apologetic power of the fully consistent Preterist view. You guys need to take a deep breath and dive into the continued development of the consistent Preterist system and its resultant worldview. Pull out all the 'stops' and get back into the 'interpretative maximalism' again. The next reformation for you doth wait. Go for it. Do

---

[35] Noe (BET, 196) trumpets similarly: "The bane and chief blind spot of Christianity for more than nineteen centuries has been its misunderstanding of Jesus's promised return."

[36] This confident statement also is reminiscent of various cults which view themselves as having finally brought unadulterated Christian truth to the world: the *Latter-day* Saints and the Jehovah's Witnesses (with the prophetic significance of 1914).

> you want to be a real reformer, or just dream about it and one day wake up to realize it just passed you by? This is your BIG chance."

Recognizing that their approach (their entire "WORLDVIEW") is contrary to the universal, historic, orthodox Christian church, Noe urges a radical shift of commitment in the church: We need "a new way of thinking, a new perspective, and a paradigm shift away from some of the traditional positions" (BET 268). Indeed, he laments that "a reformation of this magnitude, though desperately needed, is far easier outlined than accomplished. Blind allegiance to entrenched traditions stand in the way" (BET 205).

Noe deems all of this necessary because, "the Church has, since the fall of Jerusalem, been falsely prophesying a half-truth faith" (BET 219). Consequently, "it is time for this reformation, and for God's people to come out of this 19-centuries-and-counting 'deception of the elect'" (BET 219). (This sounds like the Mormon warning that "even some of the 'very elect' are deceived."[37])

With growing confidence, Noe calls upon Christians to alter the foundations of the faith: "We must be willing to admit that we were wrong and that we have misunderstood some very important, foundational aspects of Scripture" (BET 269). All Christian expectations of an end to history must be forsaken: "This fear-based, traditional, 'orthodox' doctrine has been a fool's paradise. It is an outright misconception of God's redemptive plan of the ages" (BET 269).[38]

Eventually, Noe cannot contain himself, rather boldly and naively declaring:

> "But listen — Do you hear the cry ringing over the land? It's the Prophecy Reformation's cry of 'once for all delivered!' Soon it may swell to a chorus, then to a roar! Listen! It's the sound of a faith coming together in a new harmony of perfection and power. It's a cry destined to revolutionize biblical faith in the new millennium, changing the way it's preached, practiced, and perceived. What a positive difference its discovery will make" (BET 272).

Noe laments that "others, we suspect, will dig in their heels and resist the truth of God's Word" (BET 205).

---

[37] McConkie, *Mormon Doctrine*, 194.

[38] Once again we can discern cult-like echoes in Jehovah's Witness literature, such as Charles T. Russell, *The Divine Plan of the Ages* (Memphis: Associated Bible Students, rep. [1886]).

As Stevens puts it, his preterist movement "presents an opportunity for reform every bit as revolutionary for the development of Biblical interpretation as was the first Reformation four hundred years ago.... This is one of those pivotal eras in Church history when our understanding of Biblical truth can make tremendous progress" (WH). His views offer "a quantum leap and paradigm shift in our understanding" (CPO). This is because "most of traditional Christianity has misunderstood Bible prophecy for its first two thousand years" (WH). Tim King, writing of his father's book, *The Spirit of Prophecy*, confidently prophesies: "This was the founding book of the eschatological movement that will shape the religious revival of the third millennium."[39]

Church of Christ backdrop

Many from the Hyper-preterist movement are either presently in or have come from the Church of Christ sect.[40] This sect arose out of the ministerial labors of Alexander Campbell in the 1830s (hence, adherents are sometimes called "Campbellites").[41] Some of the attitudes and convictions of this movement impact Hyper-preterism in many circles, particularly the two leading factions under Max King and Ed Stevens.

Though Stevens has formally left the Church of Christ, his theological thinking is clearly haunted by his background. He even mentions the Campbellite "Restoration" movement alongside of the Reformation as a major episode in church history! He longs for a "better understanding" of

---

[39] Tim King, "Quest Interview with Tim King: August 25, 1999 by Holy Ground Ministries." Posted on the Living Presence website.

[40] The founder and driving force of Living Presence Ministries is Max King, a Church of Christ minister. His son, Tim King, is the President of LPM. Ed Stevens graduated from the Church of Christ "Bible Institute" and preached for nine years as one of their ministers (WH, vi). Don Preston, another prolific writer, is one of their minister's in Oklahoma. We could add also the following authors: Foy Wallace, Ron McRay, Arthur Ogden, and Timothy A. James, to name but a few.

[41] Mead mentions the label "Campbellites" in his *Handbook of Denominations in the United States*, rev. by Samuel S. Hill (10th ed.: Nashville: Abingdon, 1995), 95. For an important theological critique of Campbellism, see: Robert L. Dabney, *Discussions: Evangelical and Theological*, vol. 1 (London: Banner of Truth, rep. 1967 [1890]), 314-49: "The System of Alexander Campbell: An Examination of Its Leading Points." Dabney begins with Campbellism's anti-creedalism, exposing it's inconsistency and arbitrariness.

doctrine than that found in the creeds, noting that "we must continue the efforts of the reformation, restoration, and reconstruction movements" (CPO).[42]

The "Restoration" label derives from a series of articles written by Alexander Campbell in 1825, titled: "A Restoration of the Ancient Order of Things." In that series he "argued for the abandonment of everything not in use among early Christians, as creeds, confessions, unscriptural words, phrases, theological speculations, and for adoption of everything sanctioned by primitive practice.... His plea was not for a reformation, but restoration of original church [*sic*]."[43]

We will see later how Stevens argues for putting only Scriptural words in the creeds as a means for rectifying their alleged shortcomings. We have already seen how he laments the non-biblical words that have defined the "Trinity." Stevens even approvingly cites Campbell in some places (e.g., WICW).

Stevens' concern regarding creeds also follows Campbell's pattern. Campbell once wrote: "From a full survey of the premises of ecclesiastical history, of human creeds and sects ... we have proposed an *Evangelical Reformation* — or, rather, a return to the faith and manners anciently delivered to the saints, a RESTORATION of original Christianity in theory and practice."[44] Elsewhere Campbell comments in a manner anticipating Stevens' concern for unity apart from creeds: "All creeds were theories of Christian doctrine, discipline, and government.... Being speculative, they have always proved themselves to be 'apples of discord' or 'roots of bitterness' among the Christian profession."[45]

Additional indicators

Numerous features in the Hyper-preterist movement cause concern that a cult may be in the making. Some of these may be written off as simple credulous enthusiasm, but they do fuel a suspicion that old

---

[42] Elsewhere he again mentions the Restoration movement alongside the Reformation as a positive influence in Christian history (WICW).

[43] Elgin S. Moyer, *Who Was Who in Church History* (Chicago: Moody, 1962), 72.

[44] Alexander Campbell, *Christian Baptism: Antecedents and Consequents* (St. Louis: John Burns, 1882), 18.

[45] Campbell, *Christian Baptism*, 16.

fashioned Christianity will have to go to make room for this new paradigm. Three additional matters may be quickly stated.

The Lord's Supper. Throughout Christian history the Lord's Supper has been taken as a "remembrance" of Christ who has left this world to enter heaven in anticipation of his future Return. Noe dislikes this: "No longer do we need to take communion in a somber, memorialized fashion, 'in remembrance of' Him who had departed (John 14:1-3). We take it 'anew' with Him in celebration" (BET 217; see also 270). This is related not only to their view of a completed Second Advent, but seems also to be encouraged by a diminished role for the Spirit (see comments above).

The Christian Calendar. After 2000 years of church history the new redemptive history paradigm opens the prospect for a restructuring of the Christian calendar. Noe explains: "We contend that a literal day in August or September of A. D. 70, was a third most important date in human history, along with Christmas and Easter. Call it Parousia, or Christ's Return, or Consummation Day, or something else. Perhaps future Christians will someday celebrate its anniversary as well. Dare we make less of it?"[46] (His overlooking Pentecost seems to be intentional, in light of the re-orientation of pneumatology in Hyper-preterist theology.)

A Special Bible. In light of the paradigm shift required in Christianity's theological thinking, what could be more handy than a Preterist Study Bible? Stevens mentions plans for a Preterist Study Bible in his *What Happened in AD 70?* (p. iv). Of course, study Bibles already flood the market and are not an intrinsically cultic phenomenon. We already have the *LaHaye Prophecy Study Bible* with its colorful cartoons, the *Geneva Study Bible* with is scholarly notations, and more. But here we see once again the Hyper-preterist confidence that they have the truth and they need to incorporate it into Bible production.

Importance of Creeds

Despite Hyper-preterist concerns about creeds (see "Complaints Against Creeds" below), the Scripture legitimizes creeds as a duty of the church. Christians are to "continue in the faith established and steadfast" (Col 1:23), "maintain the good confession" (1 Tim 6:12), "retain the standard of sound words" (2 Tim 1:13), "contend earnestly for the faith which was once for all delivered to the saints" (Jude 3). Christianity holds

---

[46] Noe, BET 220-21.

to a core body of theology and seeks to maintain, promote, and defend it, by developing creeds in response to such verses as these.[47]

Christians must recognize that "every interpreter has to distinguish between the central data [of Scripture] and what is derived from it. Hence every student of scripture or of the tradition has to have a rule of faith. In a fundamental sense the creed is simply the way the church reads scripture."[48] Just as individuals are called upon publically to declare their faith (without reciting the entire Bible), so must the church. And she must do so clearly, succinctly, precisely, publically, formally, corporately, unitedly, and relevantly. This is an important function of an ecumenical creed. Consequently, by their very nature "creeds are in intention catholic [i.e., universal], not sectarian."[49]

Orthodox Christianity has always declared, defended, and promoted a basic foundational set of doctrines, a core theological system. Tertullian (*ca*. 160–230) refers to several articles of doctrine that we find later in the Apostles' Creed as "the rule of faith" which he deemed is "altogether one, sole, immovable, and irreformable."[50] In his catechetical lectures Cyril of Jerusalem (*ca.* 375) spoke of the faith of the universal church (Cat. 17:3) and the "holy and apostolic faith" (Cat. 18:32), and in such a way as to closely resemble the Nicene Creed.[51]

Vincent of Lerins (d. AD 450) urged believers to hold to that truth which is "everywhere, always and by everyone believed" (*ubique, semper, et ab omnibus*).[52] By 665 the Apostles' Creed was called "the symbol of the Christian faith" by Fructorosus.[53] In that Christianity is a corporate and

---

[47] For a fuller justification of creeds from a Reformed perspective, see: Kenneth L. Gentry, Jr., "Creeds and Confessions: A Defense of the Usefulness of Creeds" in Gentry, *Nourishment from the Word: Select Studies in Reformed Doctrine* (Ventura, Calif.: Nordskog, 2008), 3–14. A. A. Hodge, *Commentary on the Confession of Faith* (Philadelphia: Presbyterian Board of Publication and Sabbath-School Work, 1923). Robert S. Rayburn, "Biblical and Pastoral Basis for Creeds and Confessions," in David W. Hall, ed., *The Practice of Confessional Subscription* (Oak Ridge, Tenn.: Covenant Foundation, 1997), 21-32.

[48] J. H. Leith, "Creeds," in *WDCT*, 131.

[49] J. H. Leith, "Creeds," in *WDCT*, 131.

[50] Cited in Philip Schaff, *The Creeds of Christendom*, 2:17.

[51] Schaff, *The Creeds of Christendom*, 2:32.

[52] Harold O. J. Brown, *Heresies: Heresy and Orthodoxy in the History of the Church* (2d. ed.: Peabody, Mass.: Hendrickson, 1984), 9.

[53] Kelly, *Early Christian Creeds*, 371.

historic faith, Lancelot Andrewes (d. 1626) noted "that orthodox Christianity was based upon two testaments, three creeds, four gospels, and the first five centuries of Christian history."[54] The three foundational creeds of the holy Christian faith are the Apostles' Creed, the Nicene Creed, and the Athanasian Creed for "in Christian history [these] three creeds from the early church have achieved particular prominence."[55]

For instance, we should note that the Apostles' Creed is "the most widely accepted summary statement of the Christian faith."[56] This creed "has the fragrance of antiquity and the inestimable weight of universal consent. It is a bond of union between all ages and sects of Christendom."[57] It is "an early summary of the Christian faith, in which all Christian churches, Greek, Roman, and Protestant, agree."[58] "It has maintained in modern times its distinction as the most widely accepted and used creed among Christians."[59]

Though the exact form of the Apostles' Creed we now use (known as the *textus receptus*) dates back only as far as the sixth century, it is a direct descendent of the Rituale Romanum. And this "Old Roman Creed" dates to 150 AD, having arisen in response to the gnostic tendencies of the heresiarch Marcion (*fl.* 140-150).[60] It reads:

> "I believe in God the Father Almighty. And in Jesus Christ His only (begotten) Son our Lord, who was born of the Holy Ghost and the Virgin Mary; crucified under Pontius Pilate, and buried; the third day He rose from the dead; He ascended into heaven, and sitteth at the right hand of the Father, from thence He shall come to judge the quick and the dead. And in

---

[54] Cited from Alistair McGrath, *Christian Theology: An Introduction* (3d. ed.: Oxford: Blackwell, 2001), 8.

[55] *EDT,* 284. See also: CBTEL, 2:559; BDT, 53; Schaff, *The Creeds of Christendom*, 1:12. A. H. Leitch, "Creed, creeds," in ZPEB, 1:1027. John H. Leith, "Creeds," in WDCT, 132. Alistair McGrath, *"I Believe": Exploring the Apostles' Creed* (2d. ed.: Downers' Grove, Ill.: Inter-Varsity, 1997), 13-14.

[56] J. Gordon Melton, *American Religious Creeds*, 3vols., (New York: Triumph, 1991), 1:1.

[57] Schaff, *Creeds of Christendom*, 1:15.

[58] CBTEL, 2:559.

[59] O. G. Oliver, "Apostles' Creed," in EDT, 73.

[60] William M. Greathouse, "Apostles' Creed," in BDT, 46. See also: Bruce Demarest, "Creeds," in NDT, 179. Frances Young, "Creed," in DBI, 150. ISBE[1] 1:627; 2:1245; MHT, 3:28.

> the Holy Ghost; the holy church; the forgiveness of sins; the resurrection of the body; the life everlasting."

In fact, the Apostles' Creed is "the old creed of Rome enriched."[61] It "differs from the Old Roman Creed mostly by its length: phrases are added .., but virtually none are removed."[62] The Apostles' Creed reads:

> "I believe in God the Father Almighty; Maker of Heaven and Earth; and in Jesus Christ His only begotten Son our Lord; who was conceived by the Holy Ghost, born of the Virgin Mary; suffered under Pontius Pilate, was crucified, dead, and buried; He descended into hell; the third day He rose from the dead; He ascended into heaven; and sitteth at the right hand of God the Father Almighty; from thence He shall come to judge the quick and the dead. I believe in the Holy Ghost; the holy catholic church; the communion of saints; the forgiveness of sins; the resurrection of the body; and the life everlasting. Amen."

The Apostles' Creed was a vitally important doctrinal affirmation of the orthodox Christian church. Over against gnostic heresies, it intentionally, specifically, and clearly asserted the relationship of God to the material order. It did so by affirming: God created the material world ("Maker of heaven and earth"); the physical incarnation of Christ ("conceived by the Holy Ghost, born of the Virgin Mary"); his historical suffering ("suffered under Pontius Pilate, was crucified, dead, and buried"); his bodily resurrection in time and on earth ("the third day He rose again from the dead"); his corporeal ascension ("He ascended into heaven"); *and* his future return ("from thence He shall come to judge the quick and the dead"). Continuing in this direction it also asserts the future, bodily resurrection of the dead ("the resurrection of the body").

Each of the elements I have listed emphasizes the *historicity* of the Christian faith over against the gnostics' spiritualizing tendencies.[63] According to Brown: "Like the doctrines of the incarnation and the resurrection, the doctrine of the Second Coming places the spirit and divine in direct, intimate contact with the human and fleshly. Marcion did not believe in a real incarnation, and consequently there was no logical

---

[61] Kelly, *Early Christian Creeds*, 101. Cf. Kurt Alan, *History of Christianity from the Beginnings to the Threshold of the Reformation* (Philadelphia: Fortress, 1985), 117.

[62] Joseph T. Lienhard, "Apostles' Creed," in DHT, 22.

[63] Oliver, "Apostles' Creed," in EDT, 73; and G. W. Bromiley, "Creed, creeds," in EDT, 284.

place in his system for a real Second Coming."[64] The gnostic assault was so relentless, the threat so real that, according to creedal scholar J. N. D. Kelly, several items in the earliest creeds were "on the way to becoming stereotyped," recurring "with persistent regularity and in language which is more or less fixed," including (most significantly for our purposes) "His future coming to judge the living and dead."[65]

The Nicene Creed (more accurately: Nicaeno-Constaninopolitan Creed) expands on the doctrinal affirmations contained in the Old Roman/Apostles' Creed, especially filling out the doctrine of the deity of Christ. For our purposes we should note this creed's reiterating Christ's future coming and the resurrection of the dead: "He suffered and was buried; and the third day He rose again, according to the Scriptures; and ascended into heaven, and sitteth on the right hand of the Father; and He shall come again, with glory, to judge the living and the dead ... and we look for the resurrection of the dead."

Noting once again the concern for a material conception of the historical elements of the Christian faith, the Athanasian Creed reads in part: "For as the reasonable soul and flesh is one man, so God and man is one Christ; who suffered for our salvation, descended into hell, rose again the third day from the dead; He ascended into heaven, He sitteth on the right hand of the Father, God Almighty; from thence He shall come to judge the living and the dead. At whose coming all men shall rise again with their bodies."

Consequently, as McGrath notes, "whatever may divide one group of Christians from another, the creeds provide a summary of the points which unite them,"[66] that is, the theological foundations of our faith. Stevens seems to believe that the creeds were designed to establish *institutional* unity, incorporating all believers into one historical structure, or at least removing institutional barriers between denominations. Because of this mistaken conception, he objects: "But unity never really came. Maybe it was because they placed too much authority and too many expectations upon the creeds" (CPO). Actually creeds do unite Christians in a *body of faith* (Christianity is distinguished from non-Christians and from heretics by the creedal summaries of the faith) even

---

[64] Brown, *Heresies*, 65.
[65] Kelly, *Early Christian Creeds,* 94-95.
[66] McGrath, *Christian Theology*, 311.

though we exist in various separate ecclesiastical communions.[67] Ultimately, there is only one body of Christ.

As McGrath ably argues: "doctrine thus seeks to preserve the identity of the church,"[68] for "the concept of 'reception' is of central importance to the concept of doctrine, in that a community is involved in the assessment of whether a decision, judgment, or theological opinion is consistent with their corporate understanding of the Christian faith. Doctrine is communally authoritative teaching regarded as essential to the identity of the Christian community."[69]

Not only does Scripture oblige the church to declare its faith to the world, but, as Packer observes, "the idea of orthodoxy became important in the church in and after the second century, through conflict first with Gnosticism and then with Trinitarian and Christological errors. The preservation of Christianity was seen to require the maintenance of orthodoxy in these matters. Strict acceptance of the 'rule of faith' (*regula fidei*) was demanded as a condition of communion, and creeds explicating this 'rule' were multiplied."[70] In the third century of the Christian era, a great influx of converts from paganism entered the folds of the church. As with the Gnostic crisis earlier, the church's doctrinal foundations were once again in danger of corrosion, hence the formulation of more detailed creeds.[71]

Hyper-preterists tend to muddy the waters by misdirected complaints generated out of confused reasoning. For instance, in a paper wherein Stevens objects to my endorsing the ecumenical creeds over against Hyper-preterism, he (mistakenly) argues that I breach my subscription to the Westminster Confession of Faith. He then complains that Gentry "still believes Scripture predicted the return of Christ and the other eschatological events, but *he reinterprets the time and nature of the fulfillment of those events. He has added his own 'interpretations and applications' of the time and nature of fulfillment*"(RGA; emphasis mine).

Let us note what Stevens is doing: (1) He is arguing as if my belief in a future, bodily return of Christ is my "own 'interpretation.'" This is abso-

---

[67] For a helpful distinction between *institutional* unity and *spiritual* (doctrinal) unity, see: Dabney, *Discussions: Evangelical and Theological*, 1:323-325.

[68] McGrath, *Studies in Doctrine*, 266.

[69] McGrath, *Studies in Doctrine*, 267.

[70] J. I. Packer, "Orthodoxy," in EDT, 808.

[71] Kelly, *Early Christian Creeds*, 100.

lutely mistaken and is contrary to the whole point of my referring to the creeds: The view I hold is that of the historic Christian church throughout the ages. And (2) he is illustrating his complaint by imagining that I breach the Westminster Confession of Faith to which I subscribe — which I do not (see my response under "Complaints Against Creeds"). His stumbling and confusion here is symptomatic of all of his writings that I have seen, and it is a reason I generally do not bother responding.

Attempting to overthrow the creedal convictions of the Christian faith, Hyper-preterists argue such things as follows: "The subject of eschatology was never debated by any of the ecumenical councils" (RGA). "There wasn't a uniform position on every doctrine in early tradition" (CPO). Traditional Christians "built a creedal fence to lock out heresy, but they didn't realize they built their own prison walls.... Nothing is left in the realm of opinion for future study and better understanding" (WICW).

None of these complaints is valid. Actually, the basic eschatology of the creeds (a future bodily return of Christ and a bodily resurrection) was placed in them as a response to Gnosticism and its denial of the significance of the material realm. By placing these elements in the creeds, the early church plainly established the basics of eschatology while avoiding the details of millennial systems. These basics were frequently and amply studied by the fathers before coming to the councils and required no further debate. Stevens' argument is not only irrelevant, but simply confuses unsuspecting readers who think a point has been scored. Furthermore, how does the fact that there was no "uniform position on every doctrine" discount the fact there was a uniform position on *some* doctrines (this is the informal logical fallacy of hasty generalization).

And how does the establishing of a bare bones eschatology imply that "nothing is left in the realm of opinion for future study and better understanding" (WICW)? That simply does not make sense: many items of eschatological interest have been left outside of creedal constraints for further elucidation (for instance, each of the three major millennial views can affirm the ecumenical creeds but still debate the finer points of millennial systems). Hyper-preterists need to understand that "creeds, as they emerged historically, were never intended to be comprehensive summaries of the Christian faith in all aspects."[72] They were brief "hall-marks of the faithful, distinguishing them from nonbelievers and

---

[72] Kelly, *Early Christian Creeds*, 165.

heretics."[73] Neither a creed nor a confession is "a commentary on the whole of Scripture nor is it a systematic theology."[74]

The Deviations from Creeds

To confuse matters even more, after decrying creedalism many Hyper-preterists ultimately claim to be creedal. In Stevens' response to me, he writes: "Gentry and I both subscribe to the same list of biblical events and doctrines in the creeds. The difference is the time and nature of fulfillment 'interpretations' that have been applied to those doctrines" (RGA). Noe concurs: "The preterist [*sc.* Hyper-preterist] view that Christ did return *as* and *when* He said He would and was expected to in A. D. 70, is not in conflict with, but *honors* the major creeds of the undivided church. This view is not heretical, it is biblical.... Thus, anyone holding a preterist [*sc.* Hyper-preterist] view of the Lord's return can wholeheartedly subscribe to the eschatological portions of the major creeds" (BET 214). This may assuage the fears of some Hyper-preterists who would really prefer to remain in the bounds of orthodoxy, but it is disingenuous at best.

For reasons of economy of space, I will focus on the issues of the bodily resurrection and the Second Advent, the key issues in dispute. According to Schaff: "The return of Christ to judgment with its eternal rewards and punishment is the centre of the eschatological faith of the church. The judgment is preceded by the general resurrection, and followed by life everlasting. This faith is expressed in the ecumenical creeds."[75] I will consider the resurrection first because it is rooted in Christ's (prior) historical resurrection.

The resurrection in the creeds

Hyper-preterism denies that the bodies we inhabit during our earthly sojourn will be raised again in a physical resurrection. In an e-mail to Gary DeMar and me (dated June 23, 1997) Stevens wrote:

> Paul teaches that the body (the seed) which is planted in the dust of the ground (physical death) is not the body which is to be, but that God will give the seed a new kind of body which arises out of the dust of the ground (physical death). The outer shell of the seed (the physical body)

---

[73] "Creed," in NNCD, 216.

[74] Murray, *Collected Writings of John Murray*, 1:283.

[75] Schaff, HCC, 2:597-98.

> dies and decays in the ground, while the quickened germ of life within the seed sprouts into a new kind of body fitted for its heavenly existence. That resurrection occurs at the moment of physical death when the physical body separates from the inner germ of life.

He introduced this by noting: "I take basically the same view of our resurrection body that Murray Harris does (see his book, *From Grave To Glory*)." Max King agrees: "A physical resurrection, however, is denied (and with scriptural support), but the receiving of a spiritual body at death is affirmed."[76]

Calvin deems such teaching "monstrous": "Equally monstrous is the error of those who imagine that the souls will not receive the same bodies with which they are now clothed but will be furnished with new and different ones" (*Inst.* 3:25:7). The Hyper-preterist view of resurrection (both of Christ and of believers) is very similar to the Socinian understanding. Faustus Socinus (1539-1604) believed that "the present body must die, that another new one may spring from it."[77] One of his followers, a German named Valentin Smalcius, explains: "These bodies, which we now bear about with us, we believe will not rise again, but we are taught by the apostle that others will be given to us."[78] According to Turretin, Smalcius "wishes the words of the Creed to be thus understood: 'I believe that will exist again which was flesh before.'"[79] He even argues against one Frantiziuis: "This being established, that our bodies will be glorious, it is impossible that such bodies shall hereafter exist as have flesh and blood; for flesh and blood and spirit differ in their entire kind."[80] This may explain why some of Stevens' followers have become Unitarians (the modern day heirs of Socinianism).[81]

---

[76] Max R. King, *The Spirit of Prophecy* (Warren, Ohio: Max R. King, 1971), 204.

[77] Cited in Turretin, *Institutes of Elenctic Theology*, 3:571. See also: CBTEL, 9:845.

[78] Cited in Turretin *Institutes of Elenctic Theology*, 3:571.

[79] Turretin, *Institutes of Elenctic Theology*, 3:571.

[80] Cited in Turretin, *Institutes of Elenctic Theology*, 3:571.

[81] See Stevens' admission in: Stevens, "Wanda Shirk & PIE," 3-17. For more information on Socinianism, see: David B. Parke, ed., *The Epic of Unitarianism: Original Writings from the History of Liberal Religion*, (Boston: Starr King, 1992) and Earl Morse Wilbur, *A History of Unitarianism*, 2 vols. (Cambridge, Mass.: Cambridge Univ. Press, 1947, 1952), esp. v. 1 *Socinianism and Its Antecedents*. Though Socinianism is the forerunner to modern Unitarianism, we should note significant differences, one of which is: "The genuine Socinians held firmly to the

This view of the resurrection is also close to that of Jehovah's Witnesses, who speak of "the resurrection to heavenly glory as spirit creatures."[82] Elsewhere they interpret 1 Corinthians 15 in a way almost exactly parallel to Stevens' comments above: "The apostle Paul explains that it is not the *body* that is resurrected, but rather, he likens their experience to the planting and sprouting of a seed, in that 'God gives it a body just as it has pleased him.' (1 Cor 15:35-40) It is the *soul*, the person, that is resurrected, with a body to suit the environment into which God resurrects him."[83] Of Christ's resurrection, the Jehovah's Witnesses write: "Jehovah God raised him from the dead, not as a human Son, but as a mighty immortal spirit Son.... Jesus did not take his human body to heaven to be forever a man in heaven.... God raised him to deathless life as a glorious spirit creature."[84]

Orthodox Christians can point to an almost universal adherence in the historical Christian church to a physical resurrection (which was a distinctive of the Christianity over against Hellenism[85]). We find it in Clement (d. 100), *1 Clement* 24-26; in the pseudo-Clementine 2 Clement, 9; Barnabas 5:6ff (*ca.* 107); 21:1; Justin Martyr (100–165), *First Apology* 18; *On the Resurrection*; Irenaeus (*fl.* 175-95), *Against Heresies* 1:22:1; 27:3; 5:2:2; Tertullian (160-225), *The Resurrection of the Flesh*; Taitian (d. 180), *To the Greeks*, 6; Athenagoras (*ca.* 175), *On the Resurrection of the Dead*; Theophilus (d. 183), *To Autolycus* 1:7; Hippolytus (160-236), *Against Plato* 2; and Methodius (815-85), *Discourse on the Resurrection*, to list but a few. Kelly notes of the second century church that "anyone turning over the pages of the early church fathers will gain a vivid impression of the immense importance the resurrection-hope had for the second century church."[86]

By way of example, Tertullian argued for the resurrection of the very body in which we die: "The resurrection of the dead is the Christian's trust. By it are we believers" (*Res.* 1). He speaks clearly of a fleshly resurrection: *per carnis etiam resurrectionem* ("through the resurrection of the

---

authority of the Scriptures and to a very positive supernaturalism." Johann J. Herzog in *RelEnc*, 3:2208.

[82] *The Truth That Leads to Eternal Life* (New York: Watchtower, 1968), 45.

[83] N. a., *Insight on the Scriptures* (Brooklyn, N.Y.: Watch Tower, 1988), 2:786.

[84] *Let God Be True*, 38, 40, 41.

[85] Brown, *Heresies*, 31.

[86] Kelly, *Early Christian Creeds*, 163.

flesh") and *cum carnis restitutone* ("with the restitution of the flesh").[87] Kelly notes that in Tertullian "the resurrection of the flesh is heavily underlined."[88]

This emphasis on the resurrection of the *flesh* (Gk. *sarkos*]; Latin: *carnis*) appears throughout Christendom in numerous smaller creeds, such as the Egyptian creedal prayer from the Dêr Balyzeh Papyrus; the Latin creed in Tertullian's *Prescription Against Heretics* (ch. 36) and the Italian creeds of Aquileia, Ravenna, and Turin; in Carthage the creed of St. Fulgentius; in the Syrian, Apostolical Constitutions; the Spanish creed in Priscillian; and the Gallic creeds in St. Faustus of Rietz and St. Caesarius of Arles.[89] Thus, Irenaeus comments: "The church, though dispersed throughout the whole world, even to the ends of the earth, has received from the apostles and their disciples this faith.... [He will] 'raise anew all flesh of the human race'" (*Ag. Her.* 1:10:1; cp. 5:20:1).

The Old Roman Creed (the substratum of the Apostles' Creed) in its Latin form speaks of *carnis resurrectionem* and in its (original[90]) Greek version *sarkos anastasin*, i.e, "the resurrection of the *flesh*." Thus as noted above, the Apostles' Creed and the Nicene Creed also incorporate the physical resurrection as the formal, corporate, public, universal belief of the Christian faith. Written in a manner emphasizing the historic, corporeal nature of key redemptive events, the public creeds move seamlessly from the physical resurrection of Christ to the physical resurrection of believers.

No amount of special pleading — e.g., we just disagree with the "nature" and "timing" of the resurrection — can overturn the stubborn fact: *historic, orthodox, corporate* Christianity has always held to a *future, physical* resurrection. All forms of the Apostles' Creed have Christ physically dying, physically being buried, physically arising, physically ascending, and physically returning. Nor do the "difficulties" of reassembling a decomposed, burned, or consumed body hinder the infinite, omnipotent, omniscient God from resurrecting the dead. These problems have been dealt with effectively by Justin Martyr (*1 Apol.* 18), Tertullian

---

[87] See: Schaff, *Creeds of Christendom*, 2:17, 20.

[88] Kelly, *Early Christian Creeds*, 87.

[89] See Kelly, *Early Christian Creeds*, 889, 114, 173-176, 183, 187-89.

[90] See Kelly, *Early Christian Creeds*, 103-04. That the Old Roman Creed was originally written in Greek is a "practically unanimous verdict." Kelly, *Early Christian Creeds*, 111.

(*Res.* 32, 47) and Athenagoras (*Res.* 2-8) long ago, as well as by Reformed scholars since the Reformation (e. g., Witsius, Edwards, Dabney, Hodge, and Venema[91]).

The second advent in the creeds

Hyper-preterism asserts a *past* and *spiritual* Second Advent over against a *future* and *physical* one. Stevens clearly affirms: "Christ returned in AD 70!" (WH 5). Noe writes in a manner proving he is "not a professional theologian" (BET p. x) when he asserts: "Do you know what the Bible actually says about a 'second coming'? *Nothing*! Do you know what the historic creeds of the church say about it? Again, *nothing*!" (BET 204). He then laments that the historic Christian church has been "brainwashed by the traditions of men" (BET 205).

The three major creeds also establish the hope of a future, visible, corporeal Return of Christ (and, I might add in passing, the future Final Judgment). We must remember the contextual flow of the creeds: they establish the historical and material nature of the creation, incarnation, and (Christ's) resurrection, then move on to the future historic and material Return of Christ and resurrection of the dead.

In the Greek form of the Apostles' Creed, we read of Christ's Second Advent — in a specific and clear contextual flow: "from *thence* [i.e., from heaven where he ascended in his resurrected body] he *shall* come [i.e., in the future from the writing of the Apostles' Creed] to judge the quick and the dead").[92] The Nicene Creed states that "he ascended into heaven ... and from thence he shall come again, with glory [Gk.: *kai palin erchomenen meta doxes*], to judge the quick and the dead."[93]

The Athanasian Creed §§ 37-41 concurs: "For as the reasonable soul and flesh [Latin: *caro*] is one man, so God and man is one Christ; who suffered for our salvation, descended into hell, rose again the third day

---

[91] Herman Witsius, *Sacred Dissertations on the Apostles' Creed* (Rept.: Escondido, Calif., 1993; Glasgow: Khull, Blackie, 1823), 2:424-29; Jonathan Edwards, *The Works of Jonathan Edwards*, ed. by Edward Hickman (Edinburgh: Banner of Truth, 1976 [1834]), 2:194ff, Robert L. Dabney, *Lectures in Systematic Theology* (Grand Rapids: Zondervan, rep. 1973 [1878])835-37; A. A. Hodge, *Outlines of Theology* (Edinburgh: Banner of Truth, rep. 1878), 561-63; Venema, *The Promise of the Future*, 387-91.

[92] Schaff, *The Creeds of Christendom*, 2:48.

[93] Schaff, *The Creeds of Christendom*, 2:57.

from the dead; He ascended into heaven, He sitteth on the right hand of the Father, God Almighty; from thence He shall come [*venturus*] to judge the living and the dead. At whose coming all men shall rise again with their bodies [*corporibus*]."[94]

These creedal statements not only continue the material, historical emphasis of the preceding articles within but pick up on the well nigh universal belief of the ancient church without. For instance, Irenaeus alludes to the Old Roman Creed (proto-Apostles' Creed) when he states: "the resurrection from the dead, and the bodily assumption into heaven" [*kai ten ensarkon eis tous ouranous analepsin*] will be followed by his "appearing from Heaven."[95] Epiphanius (315-403) emphasizes Christ's flesh in his declaration that "the same suffered in the flesh; and rose again; and went up into Heaven in the same body ... and is coming in the same body in glory, to judge the quick and the dead" (*Ancoratus* 120).[96] The Greek of the critical statements read: *kai anelthonta eis tous ouranous en auto to so mati ... erchomenon en auto to so mati en doxe*).

Complaints Against Creeds

It is abundantly clear that Hyper-preterists deem the historic, orthodox Christian Faith in error regarding the several fundamental eschatological features contained in her creedal and confessional formulations. As Stevens expresses it: "If we granted Gentry's presuppositions about the nature of the 'second advent,' 'bodily resurrection,' and 'personal judgment,' we might arrive at the same conclusions he has. However, what if his presuppositions about the time and nature of fulfillment are not orthodox with Scripture? What if it can be shown that the historic church failed to comprehend the correct time and nature of fulfillment of biblical eschatology?" (RGA).

Hyper-preterist Green agrees: "*Could* not God have allowed such errors to exist for hundreds of years? Where did God promise His Church, implicitly or explicitly, that He would never allow her to make serious, non-fatal, multi-generational errors?" Indeed "what is the basis for the creedalist's belief that serious non-fatal errors *cannot* universally exist in the Church for centuries?" (PEC).

---

[94] Schaff, *The Creeds of Christendom*, 2:69.
[95] Schaff, *The Creeds of Christendom*, 2:13.
[96] See: Schaff, *The Creeds of Christendom*, 2:37.

Oddly enough, Stevens argues that "by using creeds to define 'orthodoxy,' they become a cause of division and exclusiveness," and "Here is an open admission that the creeds have been used to 'mark the boundary between orthodoxy and heresy.' This should never have been. Such an abuse has contributed heavily to the massive division among Christians" (CPO). Actually, creeds arose as a *response* to division and error; creeds did not create the divisions. And, once again, we see his Campbellite roots coming to bear upon his analysis. As noted previously Campbell argued that "all creeds were theories of Christian doctrine, discipline, and government.... Being speculative, they have always proved themselves to be 'apples of discord' or 'roots of bitterness' among the Christian profession."[97]

Consequently, in this section I will survey a few of the leading objections against creedal orthodoxy that Hyper-preterists urge against historic Christianity.

"Creeds do not define orthodoxy"

Remarkably, Hyper-preterists complain against using creeds to define orthodoxy. Stevens bemoans: "Since when did the label 'heterodox' (different doctrine) get re-defined in terms of conformity with the *creeds*?" (RGA). Apparently unaware of the function of historical theology, he is never able to cover from this theological gaffe, even charging that: "Gentry has put himself in close proximity to the Romanist position ... by allowing the creeds to be the standard by which we judge orthodoxy." He continues: "Gentry is out of bounds using the creeds as the basis for his decision about whether something is orthodox." Indeed, orthodoxy "must never be defined as conformity to a creed" (RGA). Responding to Mathison, Stevens comments: "Here is an open admission that the creeds have been used to "mark the boundary between orthodoxy and heresy. This should never have been" (CPO).

Casting the historic church's creedal labors in as poor a light as possible, Stevens is concerned that "a group of fallible uninspired men decide by majority vote what I believe" (WICW). He even poisons the well by observing in his first major section of one of his web postings: "'Orthodoxy' was more determined by how many bishops believed a certain way (majority vote) and by how powerful in influence they were (power

[97] Elgin S. Moyer, *Who Was Who in Church History* (Chicago: Moody, 1962), 72.

politics) than by correct exegesis of Scripture, reason, and fairness" (CPO). Therefore, creeds "are no more *authoritative* than our best opinions today" (CPO).

Another Hyper-preterist, Daniel Harden, is even more confused when he complains: Gentry's "use of 'orthodoxy,' however, needs to be clarified, for it is an extremely subjective term. For if we examine Dr. Gentry's Partial Preterist views within the framework of the 'common' belief of his audience, modern America, we find that in fact he is outside of orthodoxy, because the prevailing views are Premillennialist Dispensationalism and Amillennialism" (WHH).

Perhaps some of Stevens' error is attributable to his lexical confusion. For some reason he misconstrues the etymology of the term "orthodoxy" when he writes: "Orthodoxy (*ortho*: 'straight,' *doxy* 'doctrine') implies doctrine that is 'in line with scripture' (not 'in line with the creeds')" (WICW). Actually, the term is derived from the combination of *orthos*, meaning "straight"and *doxa* meaning "opinion," from *doxein* "to think." Thus, "orthodoxy" does not mean "right doctrine," but "right opinion" or "straight thinking."[98]

A frustrating feature of Hyper-preterist argumentation is its inconsistency. For instance, Stevens complains in one place: "Since when did the label 'heterodox' (different doctrine) get re-defined in terms of conformity with the creeds?" (RGA). In another place he (accurately) declares: "Originally the creeds were formulated to determine orthodoxy" (CPO). He even cites Schaff approvingly when Schaff states that creeds are, in part, "public standards and guards against false doctrine" (CPO). Which Stevens shall we follow in this regard?

We should note that Stevens states his conflict with the creeds as a disagreement with a "group of fallible men" v. what "I [Stevens] believe" (WICW). When we look at the issue in a mature, theological fashion though, what he has just stated confirms the necessity of creeds. For in his antithesis we are left with the careful, precise, orderly, debated, formal, corporate, public declaration of ordained officers of the historic, universal, institutional Christian church v. Ed Stevens. As A. A. Hodge perceptively argues, the real question is not "between the word of God and the creed of man, but between the tried and proved faith of the

---

[98] John Ayto, *Dictionary of Word Origins* (New York: Arcade, 1990), 376. Cf. CEOED 1:2012.

collective body of God's people, and the private judgment and the unassisted wisdom of the individual objector."[99]

Another Hyper-preterist problem is its faulty assumption that the ancient church theologians had no systematic, exegetical foundations for their eschatological views. Stevens boldly declares that "there really was no systematized 'orthodox' view of eschatology in the second and immediately following centuries" (WICW). This glaringly demonstrates they have done little work in patristics specifically or even in historical theology as a broader discipline. In fact, it is doubtful that they have read more than a few select passages in Eusebius (whom they frequently cite). By way of illustration, ISBE notes as one sample of the eschatological engagement by the fathers:

> "Throughout the patristic teaching the identity of the resurrected body with the earthly body is affirmed. Indeed, most of the biblical teaching is reproduced and developed in a broad synthesis.... Although the Fathers' millennial interpretations differed, they uniformly taught a general resurrection to life and glory for the righteous and to eternal death and punishment for the wicked. Their source of doctrine was both the NT and the OT."[100]

Harden complains against me that my "use of 'orthodoxy,' however needs to be clarified, for it is an extremely subjective term" (WHH). Ironically, Harden's complaint is the subjective one: On his view it is every man for himself in determining orthodoxy, whereas I follow common, historico-theological practice in employing the public, objective, historical Christian creeds for the purpose for which they were intended. In fact, E. H. Klotsche notes that such thinking is common in the cultic and liberal assault on creedalism: "Not only the heretical sects connected with Protestantism but also the liberal theologians of the church have raised an outcry against the authority of symbols [i.e., creeds] as inconsistent with 'the right of private judgment.'"[101]

Woods reminds us that "the 19th cent., however, saw the launching of a critical onslaught upon the creeds comparable with that simultaneously directed against the Scriptures."[102] As noted previously, Unitarians are well known for their disdain for creeds: "What Unitarians object to in

---

[99] Hodge, *Commentary on the Confession of Faith*, 21.
[100] R. A. Muller, "Resurrection," in ISBE (1982), 4:150.
[101] Cited in Peter Lillback, in Hall, *The Practice of Confessional Subscription*, 35.
[102] A. S. Woods, "Creeds and Confessions," in ISBE (1982), 808.

these or in other creeds is the implied intention to bind future generations to the ideas, insights, and literal words of the past."[103]

Consider the following scholarly observations regarding the respected historical practice of determining orthodoxy by reference to the creeds:

- Zacharias Ursinus (1534-83): Speaking of the Apostles' Creed: "These articles constitute a certain form or rule with which the faith of all orthodox christians [*sic*] should agree and conform."[104]
- Frances Turretin (1623-87): Creeds "contain the sum and foundation of the Christian doctrine and are like barriers against the errors and corruptions which can injure religion."[105]
- Herman Witsius (1626-1708): "The [Apostles'] creed is the distinguishing badge of Christianity." [106]
- A. A. Hodge (1823-86): Creeds "are for the purpose of preservation and of popular instruction, of discriminating and defending the truth from the perversion of heretics." They are "to discriminate truth from the glosses of false teachers."[107]
- James Orr (1844-1913): "It was the creed that could be appealed to as held by the church in all its great branches, and so as forming the test of catholicity." It was "employed to check the license of interpretation of Scripture of these fantastic heretical speculators."[108]
- R. B. Kuiper (1886-1966): "The question as to what we mean when lauding the Christian Reformed church for its orthodoxy requires a further answer. We mean that it adheres to that interpretation of the Bible at which the historic Christian church has arrived under the illumination of the Holy Spirit, the Spirit of truth.... At different times the illuminated church has formulated the truth in documents known as creeds. For example, there are the ancient ecumenical creeds known as the *Apostles' Creed,* the *Nicene Creed,* and the *Athanasian Creed*."[109]

---

[103] Harry B. Scholefield, ed., *A Pocket Guide to Unitarianism* (Boston: Beacon, 1954), 1.

[104] Zacharias Ursinus, *Commentary of Dr. Zacharias Ursinus on the Heidelberg Catechism*, trans. by G. W. Williard (2d. 2d.: Phillipsburg, N.J.: Presbyterian and Reformed, rep. n.d. [1852]), 117.

[105] Turretin, *Institutes of Elenctic Theology*, 3:283.

[106] Witsius, *Sacred Dissertations on the Apostles' Creed*, xxxii.

[107] Hodge, *Outlines in Theology*, 113, 114.

[108] James Orr, "Apostles' Creed," in ISBE (1929), 1:204.

[109] R. B. Kuiper, *To Be or Not to Be Reformed* (Grand Rapids: Zondervan, 1959), 25, 26.

- Williston Walker (1860-1922): "The use of creeds as tests of orthodoxy by the councils, such as Nicaea in 325, gave added prominence to the declaratory type."[110]
- William Kelly (1960): "With the development of heretical teaching, however, there was a natural tendency to use the creeds as a test of catholic orthodoxy. This is the most likely explanation of the use of the Latin term *symbolum* for a creed. It is a token by which the true Christian faith can be known from the infidel or heretic."[111]
- William Barclay (1967): "Although the Christian has a wide field in which to move, there are necessarily limits. Unquestionably the Gnostics would have called themselves Christians; unquestionably the Ranters who stressed Christian liberty and freedom considered themselves as more Christian than the Church; but equally unquestionably neither the Gnostics nor the Ranters were Christian. A creed is necessary simply that a man may test his own faith and thought by the faith and thought of the universal Church." And then on the next page he continues: "It might almost be true to say paradoxically that creed can define heresy but not faith."[112]
- J. N. D. Kelly (1972): In his important study, the first section in chapter 7 is titled: "1. Creeds as Tests of Orthodoxy."[113]
- A. H. Leitch (1976): A creed "is to give a testimony to those universal beliefs which bind the whole Church, not only in the day in which it was written but through the history of the Church.... In a negative sense they exclude all those doctrines which are looked upon as false or heretical."[114]
- William S. LaSor (1982): "Heresy arises when a party develops around a particular leader ... whose divergent opinion opposes some common teaching of the Church."[115]
- A. S. Wood (1982): "A creed was intended as a compendious statement of Christian faith and a criterion by which error could be exposed." Creeds "were concerned largely with safeguarding the faith against

---

[110] Williston Walker, *A History of the Christian Church* (3d. ed.: New York: Charles Scribner's Sons, 1970), 59.

[111] William Kelly, "Creed, Creeds," in WDT, 147.

[112] William Barclay, *The Apostles' Creed* (rev. ed.: Louisville, Kent.: Westminister John Knox, 1998 [1967]), 6, 7.

[113] Kelly, *Early Christian Creeds*, 205.

[114] A. H. Leitch, "Creed, Creeds," in ZPEB, 1:1025.

[115] William Sanford LaSor, "Heresy," in ISBE (1982), 2:685.

error" and "have been employed as a criterion by which orthodoxy may be distinguished from heresy."[116]

- Harold O. J. Brown (1984): "Orthodoxy is supposed to be the traditional, timeless faith of the whole church, while heresy is the error of a faction."[117]
- Geoffrey Bromiley (1984): Creeds "function as a key to the proper understanding of Scripture (Tertullian) and as tests of orthodoxy for the clergy."[118]
- Jack B. Rogers (1997): "Creeds intend to describe the faith of the whole, undivided Christian Church.... They clarify the identity of the community by demarcating orthodoxy and rejecting heresy." So "when differing interpretations of Scripture threatened the unity of the church it became necessary to identify orthodoxy (correct opinion) and differentiate it from heresy (choosing another way)."[119]
- David F. Wright (1997): "Heresy. The rejection or distortion of a major element of Christian doctrine, particularly as defined in the church's creeds and confession."[120]
- Robert Rayburn (1997): "Creeds serve a variety of purposes in the life of the church. They are a testimony of the church's belief to the world; ... they form a bulwark against the intrusion of error by providing a standard of orthodoxy and a test for office-bearers."[121]
- Alistair E. McGrath (1997): Under the heading "The Purpose of Creeds" McGrath states "three main purpose," one of which is "as a test of orthodoxy for Christian leaders."[122]

In fact, concerning the Apostles' Creed we read the following comments by biblical and theological scholars: "The [Apostles'] creed has been appealed to by all branches of the church as a test of authentic faith."[123] It "allows us to *recognize and avoid inadequate or incomplete versions of Christianity*."[124] It "lists a series of central doctrines, which may be regarded as fundamental to the Christian faith ... [and] has served ... as a

---

[116] A. S. Wood, "Creeds and Confessions," in ISBE (1982), 1:807, 812.

[117] Brown, *Heresies*, 9.

[118] Bromiley, "Creed, creeds," in EDT, 284.

[119] Jack B. Rogers, in ERF, 91.

[120] David F. Wright, "Heresy," in McKim, ERF, 172.

[121] Robert Rayburn, in David W. Hall, ed., *The Arrogance of the Modern: Historical Theology Held in Contempt* (Oak Ridge, Tenn.: Calvin Institute, 1997), 21.

[122] McGrath, *"I Believe,"* 14.

[123] NIBD, 263.

[124] McGrath, *Studies in Doctrine*, 314.

test of orthodoxy for Christian leaders."[125] In his discussion of the development of the Apostles' Creed, Witsius notes that "in order to distinguish the doctrine of the church from heresy, and the true sons of the church from heretics and their followers, several articles were gradually added." He even states that "it is now so generally received in Christendom, that the man who wantonly rejects it, ought not to be esteemed a Christian."[126]

The same is true of the Nicene Creed: As is well-known, Walker notes that "the Nicene Creed of 325 was drawn up to counter the Arian challenge."[127] McGrath comments that it "was first and foremost a definition of orthodox faith for bishops."[128] Murray declares that it was a "bulwark against heresy."[129] The council of Nicea, according to Schaff, was "the most important event of the fourth century" because it effected an "intellectual victory over a dangerous error."[130] And of the Athanasian Creed.[131] On and on we could go multiplying authorities.

The Hyper-preterist complaint against using creeds to determine orthodoxy is embarrassingly naive, frustratingly contradictory, and surprisingly ill-founded.

"We have no creed but Scripture"

A favorite complaint of all anti-creedalist splinter groups and cults is the cry: "No creed but Scripture!" Hyper-preterists proudly declare: "Orthodoxy is determined by *sola scriptura* not by creeds" (WICW). Though all evangelical, creedal Christians recognize the *ultimate* and *unique* authority of Scripture as the very word of God, this popular maxim proposes an impossible goal (as we shall see). In fact, it is torn with dialectical tension, for the declaration "no creed but Scripture" is a creed itself.

Stevens argues against my use of creeds when I confront the novel Hyper-preterist doctrine. He complains: Gentry "doesn't trust his fellow

---

[125] McGrath, *Studies in Doctrine*, 313-14.

[126] Witsius, *Sacred Dissertations on the Apostles Creed*, 1:12, 14.

[127] James B. Walker, "Niceno-Constantinopolitan Creed," in DHT, 397.

[128] Kelly, *Early Christian Creeds*, 255.

[129] Murray, *Collected Writings of John Murray*, 281.

[130] Schaff, HCC, 3:631.

[131] ISBE[1] 4:3021-22; Elgin S. Moyer, *Who Was Who in Church History* (Chicago: Moody, 1962), 17, 21-22.

Christian to arrive at truth" (WICW). Of course, we should remember that it was Stevens himself who warned "most of traditional Christianity has misunderstood Bible prophecy for its first two thousand years" (WH, 5). Why should I trust Ed Stevens if he can't trust millions of Christians and thousands of theologians over hundreds of years? Berkhof has well noted that to urge "no creed but the Bible" is a "virtual denial of the guidance of the Holy Spirit in the past history of the Church."[132]

Stevens also charges that Gentry "assumes that the creeds have been thoroughly 'tried and proved'.... No more trials by the tests of time are necessary?" (WICW). Actually, we don't "assume" the creeds have been "tried and proved," we point to historical theology and exegetical findings to show that they have.

In a statement utterly perplexing to me, Stevens argues about my conviction that the creeds do not contain eschatological error: "It seems that Gentry does not even want to consider that possible. He is content with creedal interpretations" (RGA). Why this befuddles me is because he makes this statement in his response to my short article in which I provide *twelve* theological arguments against Hyper-preterism, only *one* of which is my creedal concern. Furthermore, I have several books and numerous articles published that provide arguments for the historic, orthodox Christian view of eschatology.

Stevens presents a false-antithesis when he writes: "which would you rather throw out the window, the New Testament writings, or the creeds?" (cited in BET 216). Elsewhere he re-asserts this false dilemma: "We must decide which is the right course of action: sacrifice the inspiration of Jesus and the NT writers in order to maintain the integrity of the uninspired creeds and Church fathers, or preserve the inspiration of Jesus and the NT and impeach the fallible interpretations and applications of the historic church" (WH 5–6). These rally-cries are superficially compelling to those unschooled in logic and theology.

But the more accurate antithesis would really be: Which would you rather throw out the window: the novel theological position of Ed Stevens or the convictions of the universal Christian Church of all ages? As noted before, Hodge reminds us that:

> the real question between the church and the impugners of creeds, is not, as the latter often pretend, between the word of God and the

---

[132] Louis Berkhof, *Systematic Theology* (new ed.: Grand Rapids: Eerdmans, 1996), 32.

> creed of man, but between the tried and proved faith of the collective body of God's people, and the private judgment and the unassisted wisdom of the individual objector.[133]

In fact, in the literature of Jehovah's Witnesses we read a Stevens-like complaint: "To arrive at truth we must dismiss religious prejudices from heart to mind. We must let God speak for himself.... To let God be true means to let God have the say as to what is the truth that sets men free. It means to accept his word, the Bible, as the truth. Our appeal is to the Bible for truth." This same book spurns creeds as "man-made traditions," "the precepts of men," and "opinions."[134]

In this regard, evangelical historian Nathan Hatch writes:

> The first Americans to underscore the right of private judgment in handling the Scriptures were, oddly enough, ministers who opposed the evangelical tenets of the First Great Awakening.... Theological liberals became increasingly restive with strict creedal definitions of Christianity.... Well into the nineteenth century, rational Christians, many of whom swelled the ranks of denominations such as the Unitarians and the Universalists, argued against evangelical orthodoxy by appealing to the Bible.... Charles Beecher defended his rejection of his father Lyman's orthodoxy by renouncing 'creed-power' and raising the banner of "the Bible, the whole Bible, and nothing but the Bible."[135]

In the liberal/conservative struggle in Northern Baptist circles early in the Twentieth Century, one fundamentalist leader, William Bell Riley, proposed in 1922 a confession "be adopted as a creed." But this "was defeated by a two-to-one margin in favor of a proposal making the New Testament the only ground of faith and practice. By 1926, militant Baptist fundamentalists knew the battle was lost."[136]

Berkhof notes that the denial of creeds "represents unwarranted individualism in the development and formulation of the truth, an exaggerated notion of a single individual, or of the church of a single generation to rear *de novo* a better structure of religious truth than the time-honored system of the past."[137]

---

[133] Hodge, *A Commentary of the Confession of Faith*, 21.

[134] *Let God Be True*, 9, 11.

[135] Hatch, "Sola Scriptura and Novus Ordo Seclorum," 164.

[136] Martin E. Marty and R. Scott Appleby, eds., *Fundamentalisms Observed* (Chicago: University of Chicago Press, 1991), 24.

[137] Berkhof, *Systematic Theology*, 32.

Stevens, in CPO, even argues "if we must have an authoritative creed, let it be Christ" — whatever that means. In this he agrees with the liberal "Confession of 1967" from the United Presbyterian Church. In that confessional document, we discover that Article 9.03 reads: "Obedience to Jesus Christ alone identifies the one universal church and supplies the continuity of its tradition. This obedience is the ground of the church's duty and freedom to reform itself in life and doctrine as new occasions, in God's providence, demand." A thin line separates this liberal sentiment from that of the Hyper-preterist.

"Creeds are not infallible"

Whenever orthodox Christians challenge Hyper-preterists regarding their orthodoxy, the Hyper-preterist reflex is to make overstated claims regarding our creedal convictions. For instance, Stevens writes: "Gentry seems to ascribe virtual infallibility (inspiration) to the creeds. This should make any true Reformer shudder" (RGA). The moderating word "seems" is dropped and the charge becomes more exaggerated in his booklet, *What Happened in A. D. 70?*: "Creedalists believe the creeds are untouchable. They assume that the creeds are infallibly correct, and therefore absolutely authoritative. They are thereby imputing inspiration to the creeds" (WH 6).

After declaring 2000 years of "traditional Christianity" mistaken, Stevens laments: "Those who believe the creeds are infallible and inspired and authoritative will take special offense at this" (WH 5). Thus, "it seems strange to me that any reformer would put a human document on a par with Scripture" (CPO).

Of course, no evangelical, creedally-based Christian will "ascribe virtual infallibility (inspiration)" to creeds themselves. Nor do they "put a human document on a par with Scripture." And this is why Hyper-preterists never quote any of their opponents as declaring such: *there are no such quotes available*. The assertion is simply not true. Rather, orthodox Christians believe that *doctrines* contained in the creeds are the doctrines of *Scripture*, and therefore the doctrines are deemed infallibly certain because they derive from God.

Actually, understanding the original meaning of the word "creed" may be helpful for dispelling this anti-creedal concern. The English word *creed* is derived from the Latin *credo,* which simply means: "I believe." A creed, then, is a statement of faith. As such, a creed no more diminishes the authority of God's Word than do statements such as "I believe in God" or

"I believe in the resurrection of Christ." As a matter of fact, such statements *are* creeds — albeit brief, informal ones. Anyone who thinks of God in a particular way has "encreeded" a view of God, whether or not he reduces this "creed" to writing. Surely this in no way diminishes the primacy or the centrality of the Bible.

Ironically, we agree with one point of what serves as Stevens' *personal creed*: He believes in "the inspiration of Jesus and the NT writers" and that "our faith cannot stand if the inspired NT apostles and prophets made a mistake" (WH 5, 6). Again, we must remember that all of this debate is over the difference between the formal, unified mind of the church through the centuries over against a small band of untrained theological innovators in the present.

"The Reformation principle contradicts creedalism"

Stevens informs his readers that he has left the Church of Christ sect and "embraced Reformed covenant theology" (WH, vi). In resisting creeds, he plays upon Reformed sympathies: "In answer to their question about 'what shall we use' if we don't use the creeds, I suspect the best Protestant and Reformed answer to that should be *sola Scriptura* and *tota Scriptura*! Using creeds to determine orthodoxy has been a major problem all along" (CPO).

Stevens laments the (alleged) surrender of the Reformational approach, noting that "many of our forefathers gave their blood to advance the reformation plea of *Sola Scriptura* and *Tota Scriptura* (only Scripture and all of Scripture). They protested the pope's and the catholic church's insistence on possessing equal authority with scripture. If we give the creeds similar authoritative status, we unconditionally surrender to the pope's claims, and contradict much of what the Reformation stood for" (CPO). Green agrees: "how is it that the creedalists believe that they are not acting in a manner incompatible with the Reformation principle of *sola scriptura*?" (PEC).

But is a creedal determination of orthodoxy anti-Reformational? Not in the least! In fact, it is an expression of high Reformational principle. Reformed theologian John Murray observes a commonly recognized phenomenon: "The most prolific period of creedal composition was the Reformation."[138] Christian historian Mark Noll speaks of "the great outpouring of confessions in the first century and one-half of Protes-

---

[138] Murray, *The Collected Writings of John Murray*, 1:281.

tantism."[139] Indeed, Rogers notes that "of all the Protestant traditions, the Reformed has been the most prolific in producing confessional documents."[140] Richard Müller agrees: "The Reformation of the sixteenth century was, without qualification, the great era of Protestant confessional theology. The writing of the great confessions of the Protestant churches was a primary manifestation of reform-impulse."[141]

Contrary to the Hyper-preterist efforts to draw away Reformed disciples with such an argument, John Jefferson Davis notes: "It is important to realize that the *sola scriptura* principle did not imply for the Reformers a rejection of all church tradition. They affirmed the value and validity of the ecumenical creeds of the early church, and in fact believed that the weight of patristic authority supported the Reformed cause."[142]

Historian David Wells agrees: "The Protestants [of the Reformation] anchored their case in the patristic period, the teachings they largely identified with, arguing that the Reformation was really a contest between patristic and medieval Christianity."[143]

Creedal scholar Kelly reminds us regarding the Apostles' Creed that "its authority was generally recognized at the Reformation, Martin Luther singling it out as one of three binding sums of belief, and both Calvin and Zwingli including it among their doctrinal norms." Elsewhere he writes: "Of all existing creeds [the Niceno-Constantinopolitan Creed] is the only one for which ecumenicity, or universal acceptance can be plausibly claimed.... So far from displacing it, the Reformation reaffirmed its binding character."[144]

Samuel Miller, the great Reformed confessional authority, has written:

> Before the Church, as such, can detect heretics, and cast them out from her bosom — before she can raise her voice, in a 'day of rebuke and of blasphemy,' against prevailing errors — her governors and members must be agreed what is truth. And, unless they would give themselves up, in their official judgments, to all the caprice and feverish effervescence of occasional feeling, they must have some accredited, perma-

---

[139] Mark A. Noll, "Confessions of Faith," in EDT, 263.

[140] Rogers, "Creeds," ERF, 92.

[141] Richard A. Müller, "Reformed Confessions and Catechisms," in DHT, 466.

[142] John Jefferson Davis, *Foundations of Evangelical Theology* (Grand Rapids: Baker, 1984), 226.

[143] Wells, *No Place for Truth*, 105.

[144] Kelly, *Early Christian Creeds*, 368, 296.

> nent document, exhibiting what they have agreed to consider as truth.[145]

Miller continues: "They must either have such 'a form of sound words,' which they have voluntarily adopted, and pledged themselves to one another 'hold fast;' or they can have no security that any two or more successive decisions concerning soundness in the faith will be alike." Indeed, of those who fail to creedally declare themselves, he says: "If they fail to do this; if, under the guise of adherence to that great Protestant maxim, that the Bible is the only infallible rule of faith and manners.., they speak and act as if all who profess to receive the Bible were standing upon equally solid ground."[146]

The magisterial Reformer John Calvin noted that theological precision (as in creeds) was necessary to "pluck the mask" from the heretic.[147] For him the Apostles' Creed "sums up in a few words the main points of our redemption, and thus may serve as a tablet for us upon which we see distinctly and point by point the things in Christ that we ought to heed.... As far back as men can remember it was certainly held to be of sacred authority among all the godly" (*Inst.* 2:16:18).

Calvin also states:

> "I have no doubt, that, from the very commencement of the Church, and, therefore, in the very days of the Apostles, it held the place of a public and universally received confession, whatever be the quarter from which it originally proceeded. It is not probable that it was written by some private individual, since it is certain that, from time immemorial, it was deemed of sacred authority by all Christians. The only point of consequence we hold to be incontrovertible, viz., that it gives, in clear and succinct order, a full statement of our faith, and in every thing which it contains is sanctioned by the sure testimony of Scripture." (*Inst.* 2:16:18)

The Genevan Reformer, Frances Turretin commented that "the [Apostles'] Creed, the Lord's Prayer and the decalogue" contain the "substance of the Christian religion." He noted that the Creeds "contain the sum and foundation of the Christian doctrine and are like barriers against the errors and corruptions which can injure religion."[148]

---

[145] Miller, *Doctrinal Integrity*, 12.

[146] Miller, *Doctrinal Integrity*, 13, 19.

[147] John Calvin, *Institutes of the Christian Religion*, trans. by Henry Beveridge, 1:13:5.

[148] Turretin, *Institutes of Elenctic Theology*, 3:135, 283.

The Heidelberg Catechism asks in question 22: "What is then necessary for a christian [*sic*] to believe? It answers this question: "All things promised us in the gospel, which the articles of our catholic undoubted christian faith, briefly teach us." The next question asks: "What are these articles?" The answer given is a full citation of the Apostles' Creed. The Westminster Shorter Catechism has the Apostles' Creed annexed in a footnote to its ending. The divines explain why they do this: "because it is a brief sum of the Christian faith, agreeable to the Word of God, and anciently received in the churches of Christ."

Reformed theologian Zacharias Ursinus notes one of the several purposes of the Apostles' Creed: "That the faithful might have a certain badge or mark by which they might then and in all future ages be distinguished from unbelievers and heretics" and "that there might be extant some perpetual rule, short, simple, and easily understood by all, according to which every doctrine and interpretation of Scripture might be tried, that they might be embraced and believed when agreeing therewith, and rejected when differing from it."[149]

In a reformed debate context, Westminster Theological Seminary theologian R. B. Kuiper wrote: "The question as to what we mean when lauding the Christian Reformed Church for its orthodoxy requires a further answer. We mean that it adheres to that interpretation of the Bible at which the historical Christian church has arrived under the illumination of the Holy Spirit of truth."[150]

Murray observes that "it is a fact of history that the church in the maintenance and defence of the faith found it necessary to formulate her faith in creedal statement in order to guard the faith against the incursions of error. Can it be denied that the Nicene Creed proved to be the bulwark against a heresy that would have removed the cornerstone of Christian confession?"[151]

"Eschatology is undeveloped in the creeds"

Another important means for discounting the relevance of the creeds in the debate is the Hyper-preterist assertion that the creeds were eschatologically undeveloped. Stevens laments: "For too long we have been

---

[149] Ursinus, *Commentary of Dr. Zacharias Ursinus on the Heidelberg Catechism*, 118.

[150] Kuiper, *To Be or Not to Be Reformed*, 25.

[151] Murray, *Collected Writings of John Murray*, 1:281.

stymied by eschatological views that have not been developed beyond 2nd-century concepts" (Foreword, BET x). The problem as he sees it is that "the subject of eschatology was never debated by any of the ecumenical councils" (Stevens, RGA). Stevens boldly declares that "there really was no systematized 'orthodox' view of eschatology in the second and immediately following centuries" (WICW).

Of the councils formulating the creeds, Stevens asks: "How much had they studied eschatology before they formulated those statements in the creeds? Is there any chance their opinions were mistaken and need to be reformed or rewritten? We don't believe the futurist creedal statements came from careful enough study. It is time to reform them" (CPO).

According to Stevens "the preterist view is not anti-creedal. It could be *non-creedal* (not definitively dealt with in the creeds), but it is not *anti-creedal* (against the essence of the creeds). We certainly agree that the councils did not make any one millennial formula a litmus test. Since they didn't, it might be wise to think twice before we do it today; because it might just be ruling out the possibility of our own views" (CPO).

The last point cited can be quickly dispatched as an irrelevancy: Millennial systems are not the issue; none of the major ecumenical creeds set up one millennial system over another. Each of the major evangelical millennial systems is "orthodox" in terms of creedal compatibility, for each affirms the creedal eschatological core: the still future return of Christ, final judgment, and bodily resurrection.

A specimen of the Hyper-preterists' inability to follow theological arguments and to draw logical conclusions is clearly exhibited in Stevens, where he makes a rather glaring misapplication of a statement by DeMar and Leithart:

> Gary DeMar and Peter Leithart, in *The Reduction of Christianity* (15, 16), under the subhead, "Creeds and Eschatology," suggest that the creeds do not necessarily rule out the possibility of a basic preterist approach:
>
> > "It is important to recognize that the historic creeds of the church *do not include anything* about the millennium, the rapture, the Antichrist, or the great tribulation. The creeds mention 'individual eschatology,' such as the resurrection of the body and everlasting life. They also say that Christ will return again in judgment. *Yet, as far as the creeds are concerned, the timing of Christ's second coming is a matter of doctrinal freedom: The creeds did not bind any believer to a particular millennial position.*" [emphasis added]
>
> Is 'the timing of Christ's second coming a matter of doctrinal freedom?'" (CPO)

No one may legitimately extract DeMar and Leithart's statement from its contextual setting and apply it to the debate over Hyper-preterism. DeMar and Leithart were confronting premillennialists regarding their quarrel with postmillennialists as to whether Christ would return prior to or after the millennium.[152] The "doctrinal freedom" they are speaking of is a freedom *within creedal orthodoxy*, not *despite* it.

In a dispute with an orthodox preterist (who holds that the great tribulation occurred in the first century but that the Second Advent is still future), Stevens asks: "Is his own 'partial preterist' view any more well-supported in the patristics than the 'full preterist' view?" (WICW). Here Stevens is asking a question for rhetorical purposes — despite the fact he himself knows the answer: He is quite familiar with the "partial preterism" of various early church fathers.

In Noe's book, for which Stevens writes the Foreword, we find references to the preterism of Eusebius (260–340) and Athanasius (295–373) (BET 214). But what is worse, two pages after Stevens makes his statement, he writes: "There were a number of early writers who made significant preterist statements" (WICW), while admitting "it must be noted that the saints who made these statement were not full preterists" (WICW). Again the problem of self-contradiction plagues Stevens.

In fact, the early church fathers engage in much discussion and exposition of eschatological issues. Once again, the future bodily resurrection is a favorite topic. Irenaeus vigorously asserts the corporeal resurrection over against Gnosticism and Marcionism (e.g., *Ag. Her.* 1:17; 5:3; 5:6-7; 5:31-32). Tertullian writes an entire treatise on the resurrection: *de Resurrectione carnis* (*The Resurrection of the Flesh*), as does Athenagoras (*2d cent.*), who wrote *De resurrectione* (*On the Resurrection*).

As Brown notes, the Apostles' Creed articles on eschatological fundamentals are well thought out and designed to stand against "the first great heretic" Marcion, for "like the doctrines of the incarnation and the resurrection, the doctrine of the second coming places the spiritual and divine in direct, intimate contact with the human and fleshly. Marcion did not believe in a real incarnation, and consequently there was no logical place in his system for a real Second Coming."[153] In fact, "it is important

---

[152] Gary DeMar and Peter Leithart, *The Reduction of Christianity: Dave Hunt's Theology of Cultural Surrender* (Atlanta: American Vision, 1988), 15-16.

[153] Brown, *Heresies*, 65. See also: Kenneth Scott Latourette, *A History of Christianity*, (New York: Harper and Row, 1975), 1:135-36.

to note the difference between the early Christian conception of eternal life and the widespread Hellenistic assumption of the immortality of the soul.... The great creeds speak of the resurrection 'of the body' (Apostles' Creed) or 'of the dead' (Nicene Creed), not of the immorality of the soul."[154]

"Creedalists contradict themselves"

In a woefully ill-conceived objection against creedally orthodox preterists, Hyper-preterists make painfully embarrassing argumentative gaffes. Basically their arguments follow two lines of objections, both of which are fallacious. I will state these first, then critique them afterwards.

First, Hyper-preterists are fond of complaining that orthodox preterists themselves breech the creeds. For instance, Stevens responds to my statement that "no creed allows any other type of resurrection than a bodily one," by noting that "it could be argued that the creeds don't allow any kind of coming of Jesus in AD 70. This presents a problem for Gentry, since he does believe there was some kind of coming of Christ in AD 70. Do the creeds allow him that freedom?" (RGA). Elsewhere he repeats this charge: "Creedalists . . . believe there was some kind of 'minor' return of Christ in AD 70, with another final coming in the future. The multiple coming idea is just as much a departure from the creeds as is the full preterist view. The creeds don't mention any kind of parousia at AD 70 ('minor' or otherwise). So, if it is against the creeds to place Christ's final return in AD 70, it is just as much against them to place *any kind of coming* there" (WH, 10).

Noe agrees: "Amazingly, no creed teaches or even recognizes that any kind of judgment or coming occurred in A. D. 70" (BET 214). Gautier makes this same mistake: "The creeds reflect the one future-to-the New Testament writers Coming of Christ. The partial preterist teaches two. In reality, the partial preterist believes in a Third Coming of Christ" (PA). As does Harden: "Not one creed teaches a multiple Parousia" (WHH).

Second, a corollary charge is directed specifically against preterists of confessionally Presbyterian convictions. Stevens points out that WCF 25:6 calls the Pope the "Antichrist" and "the man of sin," then comments that:

> Gentry's denomination supposedly holds to [the Confession] rigidly.... Gentry is obviously not in "strict subscription" to the WCF, since his commentary on Revelation teaches the Beast was Nero. Why didn't

---

[154] Brown, *Heresies*, 31.

> Gentry stick with it? Who gave him the freedom to reform it? This is an eschatological 'interpretation and application' of Scripture. Is he the only one who has the right to interpret and apply Scripture in a different way than past generations? (RGA).

Gautier accuses me in this regard of "selective non-conformity" with the Confession of Faith, charging that I "pick and choose" what I want to believe (DAIS). Consequently, as Stevens complains: "If [Gentry] has the right to correct errors in previous generations' eschatological concepts, why don't we?" (RGA).

The first argument is built on a mistaken premise. It is basically arguing that since the creeds do not mention Christ's AD 70 judgment upon Jerusalem, creedalists may not believe such. The premise hidden in this argument is: No orthodox Christian may believe anything not found in the creeds. But this wholly misses the point of a creed as a *summary* of a *few* foundational Christian principles, not an *exhaustive* exhibition of the *whole* set of Christian axioms. It is as fallacious as arguing: Since the creeds do not mention the Bible, we may not use the Bible. Or, since the creeds do not mention the outpouring of the Holy Spirit at Pentecost, we may not believe this redemptive historical event occurred. The fact that the creeds do not mention the judgment on Israel in AD 70 does not prohibit us from asserting it. This is a fallacious argument from silence.

In addition, we must note the actual situation: Hyper-preterists specifically *deny* what the creeds clearly *affirm*: a future Second Advent, bodily resurrection, and final judgment. Whereas orthodox preterists *affirm* these very truths and are, therefore, not in conflict with the creeds. To clear the record, orthodox preterists do *not* believe that Jesus literally *came* in AD 70. References to his judgment *coming* upon the Jews are metaphorical statements, apocalyptic images of divine wrath poured out in history, no more literal than God's coming against Egypt in Isaiah 19:1.

Regarding the second set of objections, these are even more confused theologically, historically, and ecclesiastically. In the first place, we must distinguish between *creeds* and *confessions*. Creeds determine universal Christian orthodoxy, thereby defending Christianity against heresy. But confessions define narrow ecclesiastical distinctives, thereby demarcating denominational theological distinctives. Note the following authorities:

- A. H. Leitch: "A creed ... is concerned with the unifying essentials of the universal Church in every place and every age. A confession, on the other hand, is a more comprehensive statement of theology, more denominational than traditional."[155]

- Jack B. Rogers: "Whereas creeds are brief summary statements of the belief of the whole church, confessions are more elaborated statements intended as the application of Christian faith to one group or region."[156]
- Alistair E. McGrath: "The term 'creed' is never applied to statements of faith associated with specific denominations. These latter are often referred to as 'confessions'.... A 'confession' pertains to a denomination, and includes specific beliefs and emphases relating to that denomination, a 'creed' pertains to the entire Christian church, and includes nothing more and nothing less than a statement of beliefs which every Christian ought to be able to be bound by."[157]

Furthermore, to charge that I as a Presbyterian am contradicting the Westminster Confession of Faith is a glaring exhibition of the Hyper-preterist ignorance of Presbyterian history and ecclesiology. In the first place, Presbyterian confessional subscription, since the Adopting Act of 1729, has provided a means for declaring scruples to particular articles of the Westminster Standards.[158] Worse still, Hyper-preterists are wholly unaware that American Presbyterian ecclesiastical courts adopted an *amended* form of the Confession in 1789 and (in some circles) made additional amendments and additions in 1903. The 1903 amendment drops the statement on the Pope as the antichrist and man of sin.[159]

The form of the Confession adopted by the Presbyterian Church in America and the Orthodox Presbyterian Church was that of the 1789 revision — with slight differences: "The Presbyterian Church in America received the same Confession and Catechisms as those that were adopted by the first American Presbyterian Assembly of 1789, with two minor

---

[155] A. H. Leitch, "Creed, creeds," ZPEB, 1:1028.

[156] Jack B. Rogers, "Creeds and confessions," in ERF, 91.

[157] McGrath, *Christian Theology*, 19. See also: Mark A. Noll, "Confession," in EDT, 262-63. "Creed," in CBTEL, 2:559.

[158] See: David W. Hall and Joseph H. Hall, eds., *Paradigms in Polity: Classic Reformed Readings in Presbyterian Church Government* (Grand Rapids: Eerdmans, 1994), ch. 25: "The Adopting Act" and ch. 26 "The Constitutional History of the Presbyterian Church in the United States of America. See also: John Murray in Hall, *The Practice of Confessional Subscription*, 247-62. Francis Turretin, *Institutes of Elenctic Theology*, trans. by George Musgrave Giger, edited by James T. Dennison, Jr. (Phillipsburg, N. J.: P & R Publishing, rep. 1992), 3:283.

[159] See, for instance: "1903 Revision of the Confession of Faith," in Warfield, *Selected Shorter Writings*, 2:392-93.

exceptions, namely, the deletion of strictures against marrying one's wife's kindred (XXIV, 4), and the reference to the Pope as the antichrist (XXV, 6)."[160] Thus, I did not "reform" the Confession (contra RGA), nor do I "pick and choose" from its articles (contra DAIS).

"Creeds are constantly revised"

Providing evidence once again of theological and historical naivete, Hyper-preterists attempt to protect themselves from creedal condemnation by arguing that the creeds are continually revised. Stevens frequently argues that creeds "are constantly being made obsolete by an ever better understanding" (CPO). He muses: "If the creeds of the early church were perfect and needed no revision, why were they revised and updated in succeeding councils?" (WICW). And: "If the earlier creeds, confessions and catechisms were such infallible bastions of orthodoxy, why did the Reformers in various European countries compose new ones or make changes to them?" (RGA).

Stevens attempts to employ a statement by a Reformed historian and social critic: Gary North notes the "progress of Christian creeds" so that "the creeds have been steadily improved" (RGA). Stevens asks of various theological movements: "Why are even more doctrines constantly being developed today (such as the Reconstructionist movement, etc.)? Doesn't this tell us something?" (WICW). Noe really misses it badly when he complains: "After all, if the creeds had it all right, what was the Reformation about?" (BET).

We may quickly dispose of the objection regarding "what was the Reformation all about" by referring the reader to the previous objections regarding the Reformation principle and the (alleged) contradictions in creedalism. In addition, I would point out that Davis reminds us that "it is important to realize that the *sola scriptura* principle did not imply for the Reformers a rejection of all church tradition. They affirmed the value and validity of the ecumenical creeds of the early church, and in fact believed that the weight of patristic authority supported the Reformed cause."[161]

---

[160] From the "Preface" to *The Confession of Faith of the Presbyterian Church in America* (Brevard, N. C.: Committee for Christian Education and Publication of the Presbyterian Church in America, 1983), v.

[161] John Jefferson Davis, *Foundations of Evangelical Theology* (Grand Rapids: Baker, 1984), 226.

In fact, in Section 4 of his "Prefatory Address to King Francis" in *The Institutes*, Calvin writes of his papal opponents: "It is a calumny to represent us as opposed to the Fathers (I mean the ancient writers of a purer age), as if the Fathers were supporters of their impiety. Were the contest to be decided by such authority (to speak in the most moderate terms), the better part of the victory would be ours."

However, the Hyper-preterist argument is not just confused, its entire premise is fundamentally mistaken: The creeds were *not* revised because of a change in the understanding of biblical doctrine, they were *expanded* to include additional details for responding to *new* heresies. The later creeds left the system of truth unchanged, but the volume of truth declared was expanded. Ursinus writes: "Why were other creeds ... formed and received in the church after the Apostles' creed? To this we would reply, that these are not properly other creeds differing in substance from the Apostles' creed, but are merely a repetition and clearer enunciation of its meaning, in which some words are added, by way of explanation, on account of heretics, who took advantage of its brevity, and corrupted it."[162]

Thus, it is absurd to allege that creeds are "constantly being made obsolete" (CPO). The newer material did not render the previous theology "obsolete," but rather filled in more details. This is why, for instance, John Calvin could structure much of his discussion in *The Institutes* around the Apostles' Creed — because he agreed with it even at this much later stage of theological development. In the "Introduction" to the McNeill version of the *Institutes*, we read: "The body of the treatise of 1536 consists of six chapters. Four are on topics familiar in the history of Christian instruction and then recently employed in Luther's Catechisms: the Law, the [Apostles'] Creed, the Lord's Prayer, and the sacraments of Baptism and the Lord's Supper."[163]

"Creedalism has inherent dangers"

This final objection concerns the Hyper-preterist charge that the creeds employ man's language rather than biblical language. Apparently retaining some of his Campbellite training, Stevens expresses his concern

---

[162] Ursinus, *Commentary of Dr. Zacharias Ursinus on the Heidelberg Catechism*, 117–18.

[163] John Calvin, *The Institutes of the Christian Religion*, ed. by John T. McNeill, trans. by Ford Lewis Battles (Philadelphia: Westminster, 1960), 1:xxxv-xxxvi.

that the creeds "go beyond the mere recitation of Bible statements. They attempt to interpret the Bible." He proposes: "If it could be shown that a creed does nothing more than organize the doctrines of Scripture without adding any human interpretations or commentary to it" we would be on firmer ground. Therefore, "why not just stick with the way scripture says it, and if scripture doesn't clear it up, give freedom to differ" (WICW).

As noted previously, Alexander Campbell "argued for the abandonment of ... creeds, confessions, unscriptural words, phrases, theological speculations."[164] Campbell vehemently argued: "we adopt BIBLE NAMES FOR BIBLE THINGS."[165] We should remember that this approach even dangerously tempts Stevens to ponder the advisability of adopting the historic doctrinal formulations of the Trinity.

But the problem is deeper than Stevens' Campbellite reflex. His view labors under an remarkably superficial conception regarding the process of human understanding. We must realize that it is *impossible* for anyone to bypass "interpretation" and go directly to "meaning." All meaning is interpretation for "human language, by its very nature, is largely equivocal, that is, capable of being understood in more than one way."[166]

Beyond this epistemological gaffe, though, we should note that heresiology informs us that "the emergence of new heresies ... necessitated continuing elaboration in creedal definition and even the introduction of new terminology for which there was no direct scriptural precedent."[167] This was because "a confession of the authority of Holy Scripture combined with the particular form of words in the Scripture was not, in fact, enough to prevent fatal errors from entering the church disguised as truth and orthodoxy."[168]

Reformed theologians, such as Calvin, Turretin, Witsius, Gillespie, and Miller, defend non-biblical expressions in the creeds. Even in his day Calvin had to deal with this time-worn objection by heretics:

> Now, then, though heretics may snarl and the excessively fastidious carp at the word 'Person' as inadmissible, in consequence of its human origin, since they cannot displace us from our position that three are

---

[164] Miller, *Doctrinal Integrity*, 12-13.

[165] Campbell, *Christian Baptism*, 20.

[166] Walter C. Kaiser and Moises Silva, *An Introduction to Biblical Hermeneutics: The Search for Meaning* (Grand Rapids: Zondervan, 1994), 16.

[167] Kelly, WDT, 148.

[168] Robert S. Rayburn, in Hall, *The Practice of Confessional Subscription*, 21.

> named, each of whom is perfect God, and yet that there is no plurality of gods, it is most uncandid to attack the terms which do nothing more than explain what the Scriptures declare and sanction. 'It were better,' they say, 'to confine not only our meanings but our words within the bounds of Scripture, and not scatter about foreign terms to become the future seed-beds of brawls and dissensions. In this way, men grow tired of quarrels about words; the truth is lost in altercation, and charity melts away amid hateful strife.' If they call it a foreign term, because it cannot be pointed out in Scripture in so many syllables, they certainly impose an unjust law — a law which would condemn every interpretation of Scripture that is not composed of other words of Scripture. (*Inst.* 1:13:3)

Turretin argues that we "do not maintain that nothing is to be received which we do not find in so many words in Scripture" for "we do not seek the very letters, but the truth of doctrines and worship." Responding to the Roman Catholic objection to the reformers, he wrote: "The Arians often used this argument to overthrow the *homoousion*. The Macedonians also denied the divinity of the Holy Spirit just because it is nowhere in Scripture expressly stated that the Holy Spirit is God."[169]

Witsius on non-biblical words in the creeds: "Among articles clearly contained in the Scriptures, however, we must include not only those which they teach in express words, but also those which, to all who apply their minds to the subject, are obviously deducible from them by necessary consequence."[170] "As heretics ... retain the words of Scripture, [but] impose upon them a foreign and unnatural sense; necessity sometimes indispensably requires us, for the purpose of detecting the wiles of seducers with the greater facility, to express the genuine meaning of Scripture in our own language. Thus the Orthodox, long ago, wisely distinguished themselves from the Arians by the term *Consustantial*."[171]

Westminster divine George Gillespie (1613–49) complained that "the most damnable heretic will offer to subscribe to the Scriptures instead of a confession of faith."[172] Samuel Miller concurred:

> It surely will not be said, by any considerate person, that the Church, or any of her individual members, can sufficiently fulfill the duty in

---

[169] Turretin, *Institutes of Elenctic Theology*, 1:37, 43.

[170] Witsius, *Sacred Dissertations on the Apostles' Creed*, 1:20

[171] Witsius, *Sacred Dissertations on the Apostles' Creed*, 1:32-33.

[172] George Gillespie, *The Works of George Gillespie* (Edmonton, AB: Still Waters Revival Books, rep. 1991), vol. 2, "Miscellanies," 49.

> question, by simply proclaiming from time to time, in the midst of surrounding error, her adherence and her attachment to the Bible. Everyone must see that this would be, in fact, doing nothing as "witnesses of the truth;" because it would be doing nothing peculiar, nothing distinguishing, nothing which every heretic in Christendom is not ready to do, or rather is not daily doing, as loudly, and as frequently as the most orthodox church. The very idea of "bearing testimony to the truth," and of separating from those who are so corrupt that Christian communion cannot be maintained with them, necessarily implies some public discriminating act, in which the Church agrees upon, and expresses her belief in, the great doctrines of Christianity, in contradistinction from those who believe erroneously."[173]

Ironically, the Hyper-preterist method of objection here follows the pattern of ancient heretics, for "the Fathers at Nicaea were embarrassed by the need to adopt non-scriptural terminology to achieve their ends. Finally convinced that Arius' understanding of the nature of the Logos ... was not orthodox, they had to find a way of excluding him, despite the fact he was happy to accept any phrases culled from scripture and claims that they could and should be interpreted in line with his understanding."[174]

Eusebius mentions this when he writes of opponents to the Nicene Creed: "as to the anathematism published by them at the end of the Faith, it did not pain us, because it forbade to use words not in Scripture, from which almost all the confusion and disorder of the Church have come" (*Epistola Eusebii*, 8). Athanasius in his *Ad Episcopos Ægypti*, (*To the Bishops of Egypt*) notes of Arius: "For he too made use of the words of Scripture, but was put to silence by our Saviour" (§ 8); and "These men ... disguise their real sentiments, and then make use of the language of Scripture for their writings, which they hold forth as a bait for the ignorant, that they may inveigle them into their own wickedness" (§ 9). Later of Arius he notes: "The wily man ... pretended, as the Devil did, to quote the simple words of Scripture, just as they are written" (§ 18). In Athanasius' *De Decretis* (*Defense of the Nicene Definition*) Athansius quotes Arius as arguing: "Why did the Fathers at Nicæa use terms not in Scripture" (1:1).

---

[173] Miller, *Doctrinal Integrity*, 13.
[174] Frances Young, "Creed," in DBI, 150.

In the final analysis, we must concur with Murray: "the most basic contradictions of unbelief may coexist with a watertight doctrine of Scripture."[175]

Conclusion

A critique of any new theological construct or religious movement requires a consideration based upon the historic creeds of orthodox Christianity as an important part of the critical analysis. This chapter should provide further helpful insights for pastors enduring the disruptions that inevitably arise when a congregant picks up on Hyper-preterism. To get our bearings as orthodox Christians, we very much need a creedal analysis of the problem. Only after obtaining such a theological orientation may we move on to consider exegetical and theological issues.

Hyper-preterism is a dangerous theological movement for several reasons: First, its fundamental distinctives are directly opposed to the doctrines of the historic Christian church. Theological movements that stand against the fundamentals of traditional Christianity ought to be questioned from the very start. The interpreter or group of exegetes who agree with the historic, orthodox interpretations of the past and who find themselves in the mainstream of Christian thought should not be suspect. Rather, those who present novel deviations from historic Christendom deserve careful scrutiny. Creeds help to preserve the essential core of true Christian faith from generation to generation.

Second, we can already see at this early stage the corrosive effects the theological abnormalities developing within the Hyper-preterist movement. In that biblical truth is a seamless garment, the initial clipping of a few threads is now beginning to cause the unraveling of other doctrines. To change metaphors once again, as with so many anti-creedal movements, Hyper-preterism has loosed itself from the anchor of historic Christianity.

Consequently, it is adrift at sea and in danger of even more serious doctrinal catastrophes. Who would have known where the followers of Joseph Smith would end up when he first began to decry the creeds of the

---

[175] Murray, *The Claims of Truth*, 1:281.

church and the denominations of his day?[176] Since it struggles against historic orthodoxy, at this stage who knows where Hyper-preterist theology and the movement will end up?

Third, Hyper-preterism's danger is intensified by its ability to draw out followers through the perennial cry of the cults: "No creed but the Bible." It also feigns "scholarship" and claims "consistency" as a lure to theologically immature Christians. Van Baalen properly laments that "the cults are the unpaid bills of the church."[177] Thus, as noted earlier in this chapter, the movement is being led by men largely unschooled in the standard theological disciplines. Even within our analysis of their creedal arguments we have seen how their reasoning easily succumbs to logical incoherence, is hamstrung by historical confusion, and becomes disoriented by theological naivete. Hopefully, this analysis of many of their creedal arguments will demonstrate to those bothered by Hyper-preterism why many of us deem interaction with Hyper-preterists as frustrating, wasteful, and counter-productive.

Ironically, in the final analysis we should note that unless the (fracturing) Hyper-preterist movement develops some sort of published "creed" to secure its own health and stability, it will continue to mutate and divide.

---

[176] Michael Maudlin, "How Can a False Religion Be So Successful?," *Christianity Today* 42:7; (June 15, 1998): 5. Review of *The Mormon Story* by Tania Rands Lyon and John Lyon in *Books & Cutlure*, 5:6 (Nov.-Dec., 1999):19: "Once the most persecuted faith in the United States, the Church of Jesus Christ of Latter-day Saints (the LDS or Mormon church) has emerged as one of the fastest growing and most influential religious groups in the country. It enjoys political representation beyond its 2 percent of the U.S. population (5 percent of the U.S. Senate is Mormon, for example) and now holds assets estimated in the tens of billions of dollars. It is truly an international church; indeed, membership abroad recently surpassed that inside the United States. If growth rates continue as sociologist Rodney Stark has predicted, Mormonism will soon be the newest major world religion since Islam."

[177] Jan Karel Van Baalen, *The Chaos of Cults: A Study in Present-day Isms* (Rev. ed.: Grand Rapids: Eerdmans, 1956), 14.

Chapter 7
CONCLUSION

Consistent, Full, or Hyper-preterism is a seriously flawed eschatological construct that has become a whole new theological paradigm. Its militancy has caused much trouble in a number of local congregations that have been buffeted by over-zealous advocates.

But Hyper-preterism may have seen its better days. Though it still attracts some new followers and continues to kick up a lot of dust, more and more Hyper-preterists are leaving the ever-mutating movement. As it continues to spiral out of control, an increasing number of rebuttals is appearing in print, either on-line, in journal articles, or in book format.

Some of these rebuttals are being written by former Hyper-preterists who became disillusioned with the system. One of the most prominent men to bolt the system is Samuel M. Frost.February 23, 2016 who left in 2011. He authored several books on full (Hyper) preterism, including: *Misplaced Hope: The Origins of First and Second Century February 23, 2016Eschatology* (2002), *House Divided: Bridging the Gap in Reformed Theology* (2009), and *Exegetical Essays on the Resurrection* (2010). His 2012 book, *Why I Left Full Preterism*, is an important, brief study for those interested in seeing how the movement is collapsing.

Other well-known Hyper-preterists who have left include Todd Dennis, who was the curator of ThePreteristArchive.com. He left the movement in 2006. Kurt Simmons, former contributor to Planet Preterist, left in 2007. Bryan Lewis left in 2010. On and on we could go.

The following standard rebuttals to the system are important tools for evangelicals to consider.

Jay E. Adams, *Preterism: Orthodox or Unorthodox?* (Stanley, N.C.: Timeless Texts, 2003).

Samuel M. Frost, *Why I Left Full Preterism* (Powder Springs, Geo.: American Vision, 2012).

Kenneth L. Gentry, Jr., "Christ's Resurrection and Ours," *Chalcedon Report* (April, 2003).

Kenneth L. Gentry, Jr., "Foundational Errors of Hyperpreterism" (taped lecture available at KennethGentry.com).

Phillip G. Kayser, *Critique of Full Preterism* (Omaha: Biblical Blueprints, 2009).

Jonathan Seraiah, *The End of All Things: A Defense of the Future* (Moscow, Ida.: Canon, 1999).

R. C. Sproul, "... in Like Manner," *Tabletalk* 24:12 (December 2000): 4-7.

Vern Crisler, "The Eschatological *A Priori* of the New Testament: A Critique of Hyper-preterism," *Journal of Christian Reconstruction* 15 (Winter, 1998): 225-56.

Keith A. Mathison, *Postmillennialism: An Eschatology of Hope* (Phillipsburg, N.J.: Presbyterian and Reformed, 1999), App. C.

Keith A. Mathison, ed., *When Shall These Things Be? A Reformed Response to Hyper-Preterism*. I contribute one chapter to this work.

Brian Simmons, "Full Preterism: A House on Fire." PreteristArchive.com

Jim West, "The Allurement of Hyper Preterism: The Rise of 'Dispensable Eschatology'" *Chalcedon Report* (1997).

The concerned Christian should be aware though: like Jehovah's Witnesses and Mormons who have studied standard objections, the Hyper-preterists will have their responses. In fact, they will have their thousands of minutely-detailed responses. So the careful opponent of this view will need to keep studying. This book is only a basic starting point.

SELECT SCRIPTURE INDEX

SUBJECT INDEX

CPSIA information can be obtained
at www.ICGtesting.com
Printed in the USA
LVOW04s1009260816
501724LV00016B/88/P